ENTRAÎNEMENT AU TOEIC® READING TEST

Valérie Hanol

À propos de ce cahier

Vous trouverez dans ce cahier des exercices préparatoires, des conseils de méthode et des tests blancs conformes à la certification. Les réponses se trouvent à la fin de chaque test.

Il vous suffira de vous laisser guider !

Keep calm and smile!

Vous trouverez après chaque exercice des icônes qui vous permettront de vous auto-évaluer. En dessinant l'expression de vos icônes, pourrez ainsi rapidement identifier les chapitres à retravailler.

Un large sourire 😊 signifie que vous avez tout réussi.

Un sourire « horizontal » 😐 signifie que vous avez obtenu près de 50 % de bonnes réponses.

Une grimace 😟 signifie que le chapitre n'est pas maîtrisé, avec moins de 50 % de bonnes réponses.

Vous trouverez un **tableau d'évaluation** en page 127.

Sommaire

Qu'est-ce que le TOEIC® ?	5
Qu'est-ce que le Reading Test ?	7
Part 5 Incomplete sentences	**9**
Part 6 Complete the text	**51**
Part 7 Comprehension	**73**
Annexes	111

The Listening Test   45 minutes d'épreuve

PART 1	Photographs	6 questions
PART 2	Questions & responses	25 questions
PART 3	Short conversations (with or without visual aid)	39 questions
PART 4	Short talks (with or without visual aid)	30 questions

The Reading Test   75 minutes d'épreuve

PART 5	Incomplete sentences	30 questions
PART 6	Complete the text	16 questions
PART 7	Reading / Comprehension	54 questions

Tips (conseils)

- **Essayez de penser en anglais tous les jours** : faites la gymnastique de passer du français à l'anglais. Par exemple, savez-vous dire : Si on allait au cinéma ? La réunion a été annulée ? Si non, faites l'effort de le noter et de chercher la traduction. Constituez votre propre lexique et apprenez-le.

- Voici un site très utile : **www.newsinlevels.com**. Il propose trois niveaux de difficulté pour s'entraîner à la compréhension audio. Nous vous recommandons le niveau 3, dès le début, car vous y trouverez un script, un audio simplifié et une vidéo.

- **Pour le Reading Test**, entraînez-vous à lire des courriers de correspondances commerciales et soyez au fait du vocabulaire utilisé dans les e-mails professionnels.

Qu'est-ce que le TOEIC® ?

Le TOEIC® (Test of English for International Communication) est une certification qui permet d'**évaluer objectivement votre niveau d'anglais**, indépendamment du cadre scolaire. Le but est donc d'obtenir le score le plus élevé, celui-ci pouvant aller de 10 à 990 points. Bonne nouvelle, il est possible de la passer autant de fois que nécessaire !

Le TOEIC® permet de répondre aux besoins du monde du travail. Il permet de « booster » son CV et de se distinguer des autres candidats, quand on convoite un poste à l'international. Bien que cette certification n'ait pas de limite de validité, il est souvent demandé un score récent, allant de 6 mois à 2 ans d'ancienneté.

Le TOEIC® est également **indispensable pour poursuivre certaines études supérieures** : écoles de commerce, d'informatique… Dans les écoles d'ingénieurs, le TOEIC® fait partie des validations de fin d'études. Voici quelques exemples de scores requis par certaines écoles :

- École des mines, 800 points minimum ;
- HEC (École des hautes études commerciales), 800 points minimum ;
- Master de sciences politiques, 900 points minimum.

Tous les ans, 50 millions de certifications sont passées dans le monde.

Pour passer le TOEIC®, il vous en coûtera **entre 61 et 77 euros**.

Se préparer au TOEIC®, c'est s'entraîner comme un sportif, avec des exercices quotidiens. Envisagez-le comme un jeu, ne vous mettez pas la pression : ce n'est pas un examen. Le TOEIC® valorise l'effort et l'on prend du plaisir à avancer, car, une fois rompus à l'exercice, les thèmes, le vocabulaire et les pièges tendus sont récurrents.

Les thèmes abordés sont ceux de la vie quotidienne (voyages, loisirs, santé…) ou ceux du monde de l'entreprise (finance, achat, correspondance commerciale…). Bonne nouvelle : aucune connaissance de l'actualité n'est requise et les questions sont des Q.C.M..

La certification se déroule habituellement dans un centre d'examen mais elle peut aussi être organisée au sein de votre école ou de votre université.

Quelques contraintes administratives sont à prévoir. Il y a beaucoup moins de flexibilité dans le choix des dates pour la certification. Les dates de certification sont communes dans tous les centres d'examen en France. Les places sont limitées, alors essayez de vous inscrire suffisamment à l'avance.

Le *D-Day* (le jour J), le test dure **2 heures**, mais prévoyez 3 heures car les formalités prennent au moins 30 minutes.

La certification est composée de **200 questions** également réparties entre le Listening Test et le Reading Test.
- Le Listening Test est composé de 100 questions en Q.C.M. et dure 45 minutes. Il est composé de 4 parties.
- Le Reading Test est aussi composé de 100 questions en Q.C.M. et dure 75 minutes. Il est composé de 3 parties.

Quand vous ferez votre inscription sur Internet, munissez-vous d'une **photo d'identité** que vous scannerez. Pensez à l'apporter le jour de la certification car les photos sont souvent illisibles et l'opération est alors à recommencer. N'oubliez pas vos papiers d'identité !

On vous demandera de **laisser tous vos effets personnels** (sacs, manteaux, téléphones) à l'entrée de la salle, puis vous serez placés et on vous distribuera :
- un livret de questions sur lequel il est interdit d'écrire ;
- un questionnaire plastifié sur lequel il est aussi interdit d'écrire ;
- une feuille avec la grille des réponses à compléter.

Vous devez vous munir d'un crayon à papier, d'une gomme et d'un taille-crayon.

Il convient ensuite de noircir les cases – qui sont des cercles – de la grille de réponses sans dépasser.

Le TOEIC® change en juin 2018. Ce cahier d'entraînement est à jour avec la nouvelle formule !

Qu'est-ce que le Reading Test ?

75 minutes d'épreuve

Le Reading Test comporte **100 questions** et est divisé en **3 parties**. Il se déroule en environ **75 minutes**.

Le niveau de difficulté est croissant et nécessite concentration et rapidité d'exécution. L'ordre des parties n'est pas imposé : vous pouvez commencer par celle que vous voulez. De la même manière, c'est à vous de gérer le temps que vous consacrez à chaque partie. Attention néanmoins, à vous imposer un temps par partie. Chronométrez-vous sur un test blanc et identifiez la partie sur laquelle vous passez le plus de temps. Vous connaîtrez ainsi votre propre rythme, vos forces et vos faiblesses. En général, les parties 5 et 6 ne doivent pas prendre plus de 30 minutes (à elles deux) et la partie 7, 45 minutes.

N'oubliez pas qu'il n'y a pas de points négatifs en cas de mauvaise réponse : répondez à toutes les questions !

Il s'agit d'être stratégique et un peu audacieux ! Il est donc judicieux de commencer par la partie 7. Vous serez plus efficace en terminant avec les parties 5 et 6, qui sont principalement composées de questions de grammaire.

Voici une présentation générale de ces 3 parties.

• Part 5
Incomplete sentences

30 questions de compétence linguistique, de grammaire et conjugaison. Il s'agit de compléter les mots manquants dans des phrases.

• Part 6
Complete the text

16 questions de vocabulaire et de conjugaison. Il s'agit de compléter des phrases à l'intérieur d'un texte.

• Part 7
Reading / Comprehension

La partie 7 comporte 54 questions :

- 29 questions portant sur 10 documents uniques,

- 25 questions portant sur 12 ensembles de 2 ou 3 textes ou documents.

Elle est la plus redoutée des candidats alors qu'elle est sans doute la plus technique.

Vous aurez à votre disposition un, deux ou trois textes-supports dans lesquels se trouvent les réponses aux questions. Il faudra par exemple savoir lire un tableau comportant des horaires de trains et une lettre, puis répondre aux questions. Rien de très compliqué, mais il faut de la méthode. Ainsi vous pourrez marquer de nombreux points en très peu de temps.

Bon à savoir

• Aucun ordre imposé ! Vous pouvez commencer par la partie que vous souhaitez.

Cette partie est grammaticale. Elle comporte 30 phrases avec un mot manquant. Le mot manquant est l'une des 4 réponses, A, B, C ou D.

Vous aurez besoin de bases de grammaire solides et il est très facile d'améliorer son score en acquérant des automatismes. La moitié des phrases porte sur la conjugaison et la concordance des temps.

<u>Apprenez par cœur tous les verbes irréguliers</u> (voir p.112) et le <u>tableau de concordance</u> (voir p.12) mais, surtout, comprenez la technique, puis appliquez-la à la lettre.

Part 5
Incomplete sentences

PART 5 / TRAINING

Training

For, since et ago

For et **since** sont employés avec le **present perfect simple ou continu**.
Ago est toujours employé avec le **prétérit**.

1 This company (go) .... bankrupt 2 years <u>ago</u>.

a. ☐ gone

b. ☐ has gone

c. ☐ went

d. ☐ is gone

2 Ms Smith (work) .... in this firm <u>for</u> 8 years.

a. ☐ is working

b. ☐ works

c. ☐ was working

d. ☐ has worked

→ Voir réponses page 27.

PART 5 / TRAINING

3 The director (be) .... on the phone <u>since</u> 3 o'clock.

a. ☐ has been

b. ☐ have been

c. ☐ was

d. ☐ will be

Tableau de concordance

Proposition principale	Mots subordonnants	Proposition subordonnée
Futur **will**	if when as soon as as long as until	présent
Conditionnel **would (should / could)**		prétérit
Conditionnel passé **would (should / could)** + **have** + participe passé		Pluperfect **had** + participe passé

4 Ms Lee will take the 3 o'clock train if the meeting (finish) .... on time.

a. ☐ finished

b. ☐ had finished

c. ☐ finishes

d. ☐ would finish

➜ Voir réponses page 27.

PART 5 / TRAINING

5 If he (listen to) .... my advice, he would have signed the contract.

a. ⬜ listened

b. ⬜ will listen

c. ⬜ would listen

d. ⬜ had listened

6 If I had got the data on time, I .... the file.

a. ⬜ had completed

b. ⬜ would complete

c. ⬜ would have completed

d. ⬜ will complete

7 I would come to your retirement party if I .... a car.

a. ⬜ had had

b. ⬜ had

c. ⬜ would have

d. ⬜ have

8 He will meet the new CEO when he .... in New York.

a. ⬜ will be

b. ⬜ would be

c. ⬜ was

d. ⬜ is

➜ **Voir réponses page 27.**

PART 5 / TRAINING

9 He will send the money order as soon as the contract ....

a. ☐ is signed

b. ☐ will be signed

c. ☐ signs

d. ☐ signed

10 If we had been given more options, we .... a larger choice.

a. ☐ would have   b. ☐ would have had

c. ☐ had   d. ☐ will have

11 When the interest rates ...., the people will apply for a bank loan.

a. ☐ will plummet   b. ☐ plummeted

c. ☐ plummet   d. ☐ would plummet

Conseil

Les phrases qui suivent ne sont pas plus difficiles, bien qu'il faille trouver deux temps. Tout est sous vos yeux, repérez juste le mot subordonnant dans la phrase. Une seule réponse est possible et en concordance avec le tableau.
Go for it!

12 Ms Lee .... the memo if it ....

a. ☐ would send / is approved

b. ☐ would send / was approved

c. ☐ will send / will approve

d. ☐ sends / will be approved

→ **Voir réponses page 27.**

PART 5 / TRAINING

13. When the shareholders .... a profit, they .... satisfied.

a. ☐ see / will be

b. ☐ saw / were

c. ☐ will see / will be

d. ☐ see / would be

14. If the shipment of the office supplies .... on time, we .... our business.

a. ☐ arrive / can start

b. ☐ arrived / started

c. ☐ had arrived / would have started

d. ☐ arrive / could start

15. If the plane ...., the meeting ....

a. ☐ will be delayed / is cancelled

b. ☐ is delayed / will be cancelled

c. ☐ was delayed / is cancelled

d. ☐ would be delayed / would be cancelled

16. She .... a new car as soon as she .... a permanent job.

a. ☐ would buy / she gets

b. ☐ will buy / will get

c. ☐ will buy / gets

d. ☐ buys / will get

→ Voir réponses page 27.

PART 5 / TRAINING

Automatismes

Toujours dans le but d'acquérir des automatismes, apprenez par cœur ce qui suit.

- Expect somebody **to do** something
  → I expect you **to complete** this report before noon.
- Have somebody **do** something
  → He had his assistant **do** the job.
- Make somebody **do** something
  → They made us **work** hard.
- Let somebody **do** something
  → My boss lets me **deliver** the presentation.
- Want somebody **to do** something
  → They want us **to collect** them at the station.
- Have something **done**
  → We had this party **prepared** by a caterer.

17 Mettez le verbe à la forme qui convient.

a. They expect him (**quit**) ....

b. He wants his company (**increase**) .... his salary.

c. The consultant made us (**change**) .... our policy.

d. I didn't expect you (**achieve**) .... the objectives this year.

e. What do you want me (**do**) .... ?

f. He doesn't want John (**resign**) ....

g. The manager won't let us (**call off**) .... the meeting.

h. I usually have my assistant (**do**) .... the paper work.

→ **Voir réponses page 27.**

PART 5 / TRAINING

Mémorisez également ce qui suit

- It is the first time + present perfect ➜ It is the first time I have done such an exercise.
- It was the first time + pluperfect ➜ It was the first time I had seen him.
- It is time + prétérit ➜ It is time we left for the airport.
- Look forward to + **base verbale (bv)** + ing ➜ I look forward to meeting you.
- To agree : jamais « to be agree » ! ➜ I don't agree with you.

18 Mettez le verbe à la forme qui convient.

a. It is high time we (**lay off**) .... 10% of the staff.

b. I am looking forward to (**see**) .... you again.

c. He (**not agree**) .... with the terms of the contract yesterday.

d. It is the first time I (**meet**) .... the new director.

e. It was the first time he (**deal**) .... with such an issue.

19 Complétez ce tableau de verbes irréguliers.

	Infinitif	Prétérit	Participe passé	Traduction
a.	thrive			
b.			chosen	choisir
c.	draw			dessiner
d.		laid		poser à plat / pondre
e.			hidden	cacher
f.	hold			tenir
g.		lay	lain	être étendu
h.		rose		s'élever
i.	sell		sold	
j.	seek			rechercher
k.		shrank		
l.	sink			

➜ **Voir réponses page 28.**

PART 5 / TRAINING

 20 Trouvez le nom issu du verbe. Un indice : complétez par -al, -ment, -ation, ou rien et, attention, le radical peut changer.

    a. to renew   → the ....

    b. to refuse   → the ....

    c. to accuse   → the ....

    d. to confine   → the ....

    e. to explain   → the ....

    f. to claim   → the ....

    g. to approve   → the ....

    h. to imagine   → the ....

    i. to implement   → the ....

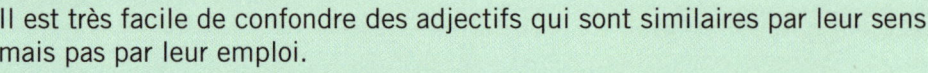

Il est très facile de confondre des adjectifs qui sont similaires par leur sens mais pas par leur emploi.

Certains décrivent une personne : ces adjectifs se terminent par **-ed**.

→ I am very much interest**ed** in history.

D'autres décrivent une chose et se terminent par **-ing**.

→ That textbook is very interest**ing**.

→ **Voir réponses page 28.**

 **Entourez la bonne réponse.**

a. The meeting is so **bored** / **boring**.

b. Jenny is **bored** / **boring** to death.

c. I am really **amazing** / **amazed** by the speech.

d. It is an **amazing** / **amazed** situation.

e. We had a **tiring** / **tired** journey.

f. I yawn when I am **tiring** / **tired**.

g. The last minutes of the game were **exciting** / **excited**.

h. The reps are **exciting** / **excited** about the new product.

Les modaux + base verbale

	présent			futur/prétérit	
POUVOIR / SAVOIR	présent →	**CAN**	futur →	**WILL BE ABLE TO**	
			prétérit →	**COULD**	
DEVOIR / ÊTRE OBLIGÉ DE	présent →	**MUST**	futur →	**WILL HAVE TO**	
			prétérit →	**HAD TO**	
TOUS LES VERBES AU FUTUR	→	**WILL**			
TOUS LES VERBES AU CONDITIONNEL	→	**WOULD**			

sauf ↓ / sauf ↓

DEVOIR AU CONDITIONNEL ↓ **SHOULD OU OUGHT TO**

POUVOIR AU CONDITIONNEL ↓ **COULD**

→ Voir réponses page 28.

PART 5 / TRAINING

D'autres modaux

PRÉFÉRER AU CONDITIONNEL	⟶	WOULD RATHER ('D RATHER)
FERAIT MIEUX DE	⟶	HAD BETTER ('D BETTER)
INUTILE DE	⟶	NEEDN'T

May et **might** expriment la probabilité à des degrés différents :
- He may come. *Il se peut qu'il vienne.* (forte probabilité)
- He might come. *Il se pourrait qu'il vienne.* (il y a peu de chance)

22 Complétez par <u>would</u>, <u>should</u> ou <u>could</u>.

a. If you invested more in R&D, it .... pay off.

b. .... you do me a favour?

c. The director .... call a meeting because there are many issues to discuss.

d. .... I accept or .... I turn down the offer? I am lost.

e. Paul .... speak three languages when he was young.

→ **Voir réponses page 28.**

PART 5 / TRAINING

23 Passez ces phrases au temps demandé.

a. Tom must reply soon. **Au prétérit** ➜ ....

b. The documents must be sent at once. **Au futur** ➜ ....

c. The CEO can't come. **Au futur** ➜ ....

d. Peter can do the job. **Au prétérit** ➜ ....

Les quantifieurs

- **Much** + nom au **singulier** ou **indénombrable** ➜ beaucoup.
- **Many** + nom au **pluriel** ➜ beaucoup.
- **Little** + nom au **singulier** ou **indénombrable** ➜ peu de.
- **Few** + nom au **pluriel** ➜ peu de.
- **Less** + nom au **singulier** ou **indénombrable** ➜ moins de.
- **Fewer** + nom au **pluriel** ➜ moins de.

24 Complétez par <u>much</u>, <u>many</u>, <u>little</u>, <u>few</u>, <u>less</u> ou <u>fewer</u>.

a. There are .... issues to discuss, Let's start to work!

b. There are .... people than last year. Only 180 contestants.

c. I want .... wine please because I must get behind the wheel safely.

d. I don't have .... time left before the meeting. Let's hurry!

e. We have .... computer problems now because we have hired an expert.

f. We have .... time to dedicate to the interns.

➜ **Voir réponses page 28.**

PART 5 / TRAINING

To wish

To wish signifie *souhaiter*, mais il peut aussi avoir d'autres sens selon le temps employé.

- **Wish + prétérit exprime un souhait encore réalisable.**
  → I wish he worked more. *J'aimerais qu'il travaille plus.*

- **Wish + pluperfect exprime un regret.**
  → I wish he had worked more. *Je regrette qu'il n'ait pas travaillé plus.*

- **Wish + would exprime un désir « ardent » qui ne dépend pas de notre volonté.**
  → I wish the postman would come now. *Comme j'aimerais que le facteur passe maintenant.*

25 Complétez avec le temps qui convient.

a. I wish the neighbour (**stop**) .... playing the drums. I can't stand it anymore!

b. I wish she (**marry**) .... Paul but she married Peter.

c. I wish you (**be**)..................... here! The party is great!

d. I can't wait! I wish she (**arrive**) .... but the train arrives in an hour!

→ **Voir réponses page 28.**

Since ou for ? That is the question.

Since et **for** veulent tous les deux dire *depuis* :
- **since** + point de départ, fait marquant, date
- **for** + durée.

Voici une aide mnémotechnique : chaque fois que vous pourrez dire « cela fait », ce sera **for** !

→ Since the beginning of the week. On ne peut pas dire : « cela fait le début de la semaine ». **Beginning of the week** n'est pas une durée.

→ I haven't seen him for a week. « Cela fait une semaine », c'est une durée, donc c'est **for**.

26 Complétez par for ou since.

a. .... the baby was born.

b. .... she left me.

c. .... a century.

d. .... 3 hours.

e. .... 3 o'clock.

f. .... 1991.

g. .... a while.

→ Voir réponses page 28.

During ou for ?

During et **for** veulent dire *pendant*.

- **During + un événement**
    → Millions of people were killed during World War II.
- **For + une durée**
    → We stayed in Paris for 3 days.

27 Complétez par <u>during</u> ou <u>for</u>.

a. .... our holidays, we went to Italy.

b. We waited for an answer .... months.

c. They talked .... hours.

d. Schoolchildren play .... the break.

As ou like ?

As et **like** veulent dire *comme*. Voilà la différence dans l'usage :

- **As** est suivi d'une proposition, c'est-à-dire d'une phrase avec un verbe conjugué.
    → As she was walking down the street she ran into Paul.
- **As** suivi d'un nom a pour traduction *en tant que*.
    → As a teacher her advice can be followed.
- **Like** est suivi d'un nom.
    → My sister is like me: she doesn't like seafood.

→ **Voir réponses page 28.**

PART 5 / TRAINING

28  Compléter par <u>as</u> ou <u>like</u>.

a. .... father, ... son.

b. .... my grandmother used to say, things never happen by acident.

c. Do .... I say, but don't do .... I do.

d. He behaved .... a child.

Question-tags

Quand le verbe est à la forme affirmative, la question-tag sera à la forme négative et contractée.

On reprend toujours l'auxiliaire au temps de la phrase et on utilise toujours un pronom personnel sujet. On met d'abord l'auxiliaire, puis le pronom.

→ James spent a week on a business trip, didn't he?
→ Jenny will have a lot to do, won't she?
→ You didn't like the presentation, did you?
→ John commutes everyday, doesn't he?
→ Erik is German, isn't he?

NB : → Let's resume work, shall we?

→ Voir réponses page 28.

PART 5 / TRAINING

29 Complétez par des question-tags.

a. John and Bob don't know what to do, ...?

b. Jenny talks a lot, ...?

c. Tom would always oversleep, ...?

d. The consultants have sent their reports, ...?

e. Ms Smith can't come, ...?

f. Let's call a meeting urgently, ...?

g. Mr Black went to Paris, ...?

Le passif

Le passif est très souvent employé en anglais, pas seulement pour faire des phrases à la voix passive, mais surtout pour traduire le « on » français.

Il comporte toujours – comme en français – l'auxiliaire **be** conjugué au temps qui convient, suivi du participe passé, c'est-à-dire **-ed** pour les verbes réguliers ou la 3ᵉ colonne du tableau des verbes irréguliers (voir p. 112).

30 Complétez ces phrases en conjuguant les verbes au passif et au temps demandé.

a. Paul (**reward, au futur**) .... for his loyalty.

b. All the invitations (**send, au prétérit**) .... a week ago.

c. A new bridge (**build, au présent en be + ing**).................. .

d. Emily (**offer, au futur**) .... a ring for her birthday.

e. All options (**consider, au present perfect**) ....

f. English (**speak, au présent simple**) .... in Malta.

→ **Voir réponses page 28.**

Réponses
training

c. Sans même regarder les réponses en Q.C.M., on peut sans hésitation trouver que **went** est le prétérit de **go**.

d.

a.

c. Repérez **if**. Reportez-vous au tableau : après **if**, on peut avoir soit un présent, soit un prétérit, ou encore un pluperfect. Identifiez maintenant le temps de la proposition principale : **will**. **Finish** sera donc au présent.

d. Cela semble plus difficile, mais le principe reste le même. Reportez-vous au tableau : après **if**, on peut avoir soit un présent, soit un prétérit, ou encore un pluperfect. Identifiez maintenant le temps de la proposition principale : **would have signed**. On est au conditionnel passé. Je choisis donc le pluperfect.

c.

b.

d.

a.

b.

c.

b.

a.

c.

b.

c.

a. to quit **b.** to increase
c. change **d.** to achieve
e. to do **f.** to resign
g. call off **h.** do.

PART 5 / TRAINING / RÉPONSES

a. laid off b. seeing
c. didn't agree d. have met
e. had dealt.

a. throve / thriven / être florisssant
b. choose / chose c. drew / drawn d. lay / laid e. hide / hid f. held / held g. lie
h. rise / risen i. sold / vendre j. sought / sought
k. shrink / shrunk / rétrécir
l. sank / sunk / couler.

a. renewal b. refusal
c. accusation d. confinement
e. explanation f. claim
g. approval h. imagination
i. implementation.

a. boring b. bored c. amazed
d. amazing e. tiring f. tired
g. exciting h. excited.

a. would b. would ou could
c. should d. should / should
e. could.

a. Tom had to reply soon.
b. The documents will have to be sent. c. The CEO won't be able to come.
d. Peter could do the job.

a. many b. fewer c. less
d. much e. fewer f. little.

a. would stop b. had married
c. were d. would arrive.

a. since b. since c. for
d. for e. since f. since
g. for.

a. during b. for c. for
d. during.

a. like / like b. as c. as / as
d. like.

a. do they b. doesn't she
c. wouldn't he d. haven't they e. can she f. shall we
g. didn't he.

a. will be rewarded b. were sent c. is being built
d. will be offered e. have been considered
f. is spoken.

Consigne

**Voici deux tests blancs de 30 questions, conformes à la certification.
Pensez à vous chronométrer, le but étant de passer moins de temps sur le second test.**

PART 5 / EN CONDITIONS D'EXAMEN

En conditions d'examen

Test blanc n° 1

1 Please meet John. He is a friend of ....

a. ☐ myself

b. ☐ mine

c. ☐ my

d. ☐ me

2 They have put a spotlight just .... the picture to enhance it.

a. ☐ under

b. ☐ on

c. ☐ above

d. ☐ besides

3 My partner and I .... together since 2013.

a. ☐ work   b. ☐ had worked

c. ☐ have been working

d. ☐ are working

→ Voir réponses page 39.

PART 5 / EN CONDITIONS D'EXAMEN

4 Would you mind .... in that way?

a. ☐ cooperate

b. ☐ cooperated

c. ☐ cooperating

d. ☐ cooperates

5 You'll be fine as long as you .... to send the estimate.

a. ☐ not forget

b. ☐ won't forget

c. ☐ are not forgetting

d. ☐ don't forget

6 If Paul .... more responsive, we wouldn't have missed the call for tenders.

a. ☐ had been

b. ☐ were

c. ☐ would

d. ☐ was

7 He left 2 hours ago so he .... yet.

a. ☐ should arrive

b. ☐ can't have arrived

c. ☐ arrived

d. ☐ has arrived

→ **Voir réponses page 39.**

PART 5 / EN CONDITIONS D'EXAMEN

8 He .... be back because the lights are on.

a. ☐ may

b. ☐ could

c. ☐ must

d. ☐ would

9 You really .... see a doctor, you look pale.

a. ☐ should

b. ☐ can

c. ☐ will be able to

d. ☐ will

10 If I .... you, I would call back the customer.

a. ☐ am

b. ☐ was

c. ☐ would

d. ☐ were

11 There were .... people than last week.

a. ☐ few

b. ☐ fewer

c. ☐ little

d. ☐ less

→ Voir réponses page 39.

PART 5 / EN CONDITIONS D'EXAMEN

12 **He wish he .... more time to prepare his presentation.**

a. ☐ has

b. ☐ had

c. ☐ will have to

d. ☐ had had

13 **Three .... people attended the symposium.**

a. ☐ hundred

b. ☐ hundreds

c. ☐ hundred of

d. ☐ hundreds of

14 **I wish I .... the promotion but John got it.**

a. ☐ was proposed

b. ☐ am proposed

c. ☐ had been proposed

d. ☐ will be proposed

15 **She took a .... maternity leave.**

a. ☐ 2 year

b. ☐ 2 years

c. ☐ 2-years

d. ☐ 2-year

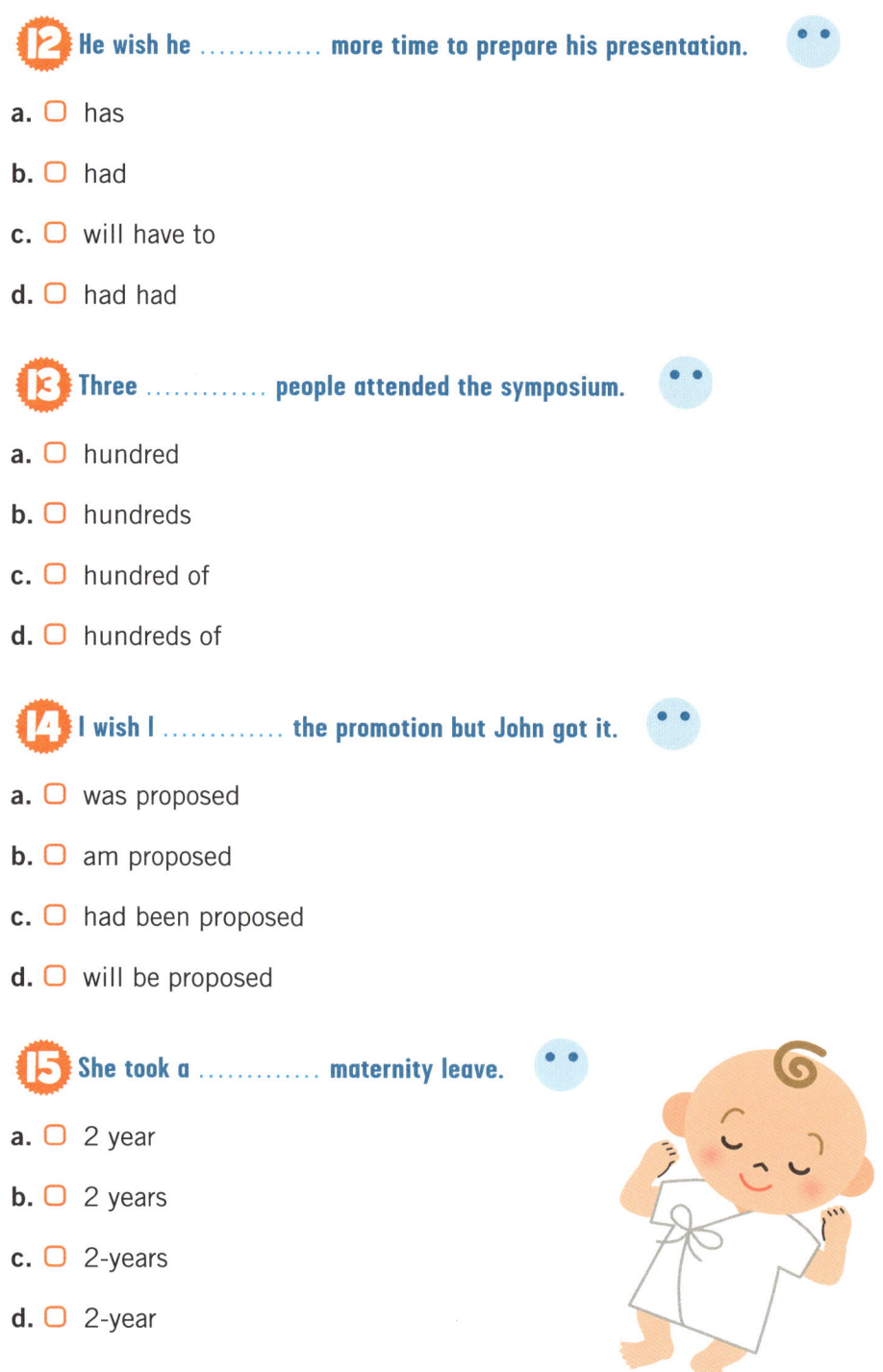

➜ **Voir réponses page 39.**

PART 5 / EN CONDITIONS D'EXAMEN

16 **Could you, please, make .... noise?**

a. ☐ less

b. ☐ few

c. ☐ little

d. ☐ fewer

17 **He has already applied .... many positions.**

a. ☐ for

b. ☐ in

c. ☐ on

d. ☐ about

18 **You .... take your car, we'll take mine.**

a. ☐ must

b. ☐ needn't

c. ☐ should

d. ☐ may

19 **John has lived in London .... 5 years.**

a. ☐ since

b. ☐ during

c. ☐ for

d. ☐ ∅

→ Voir réponses page 39.

PART 5 / EN CONDITIONS D'EXAMEN

20 You will receive a 10% .... if you pay by the end of the week.

a. ☐ rebate

b. ☐ rebuke

c. ☐ rebuff

d. ☐ reduce

21 The Prime Minister lives .... 10 Downing Street in London.

a. ☐ in

b. ☐ Ø

c. ☐ on

d. ☐ at

22 China has had an outstanding .... growth for years now.

a. ☐ economical

b. ☐ economy

c. ☐ economics

d. ☐ economic

23 I love this magazine! The September .... was great.

a. ☐ release

b. ☐ publishing

c. ☐ print

d. ☐ issue

→ Voir réponses page 39.

PART 5 / EN CONDITIONS D'EXAMEN

24 Do you think I should wear .... uniform?

a. ☐ a

b. ☐ some

c. ☐ Ø

d. ☐ an

25 .... I told you, we'll have to cut off our expenses.

a. ☐ like

b. ☐ because

c. ☐ as

d. ☐ what

26 What audience is .... ?

a. ☐ target

b. ☐ targeting

c. ☐ targetted

d. ☐ targeted

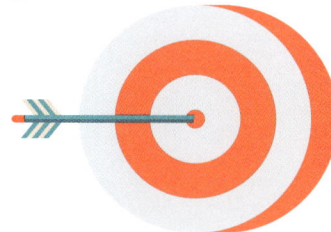

27 She spent hours .... nothing.

a. ☐ to do

b. ☐ doing

c. ☐ do

d. ☐ have done

→ **Voir réponses page 39.**

PART 5 / EN CONDITIONS D'EXAMEN

28 After .... 17 years for the same company, he quit.

a. ☐ working

b. ☐ having worked

c. ☐ work

d. ☐ worked

29 For .... information, please call the hot line.

a. ☐ fewer

b. ☐ farther

c. ☐ further

d. ☐ closer

30 This option is certainly the ....

a. ☐ badest

b. ☐ worse

c. ☐ worst

d. ☐ worstest

→ Voir réponses page 39.

PART 7 / EN CONDITIONS D'EXAMEN / RÉPONSES

Réponses
de ce test blanc n° 1

1 b.
2 c.
3 c.
4 c.
5 d.
6 a.
7 b.
8 c.
9 a.
10 d.

11 b.
12 d.
13 a.
14 c.
15 d.
16 a.
17 a.
18 b.
19 c.
20 a.

21 d.
22 d.
23 d.
24 a.
25 c.
26 d.
27 b.
28 b.
29 c.
30 c.

En conditions d'examen

Test blanc n° 2

1 The strike prevented him from .... his exam.

a. ☐ sit

b. ☐ sat

c. ☐ seat

d. ☐ sitting

2 Don't leave without .... an umbrella.

a. ☐ take

b. ☐ taking

c. ☐ taken

d. ☐ took

3 The turnover has shown a .... drop.

a. ☐ signify   b. ☐ significant

c. ☐ significantly   d. ☐ significance

→ Voir réponses page 49.

PART 5 / EN CONDITIONS D'EXAMEN

4 The new manager has been .... welcomed.

a. ☐ warmly

b. ☐ warmed

c. ☐ warm

d. ☐ warmth

5 Power in the offices will be temporarily interrupted .... the maintenance.

a. ☐ while

b. ☐ as long as

c. ☐ during

d. ☐ as soon as

6 The company made hefty profits, ... , there will be redundancies.

a. ☐ however

b. ☐ meantime

c. ☐ whereas

d. ☐ because

7 Exports to the USA only .... for one fifth of the total sales.

a. ☐ assign

b. ☐ account

c. ☐ charge

d. ☐ contribute

➜ **Voir réponses page 49.**

PART 5 / EN CONDITIONS D'EXAMEN

8 Two .... dollars have been invested.

a. ☐ millions

b. ☐ millions of

c. ☐ million

d. ☐ million of

9 Thirty candidates ....

a. ☐ have shortlist

b. ☐ have shortlisted

c. ☐ have been shortlisted

d. ☐ has been shortlisted

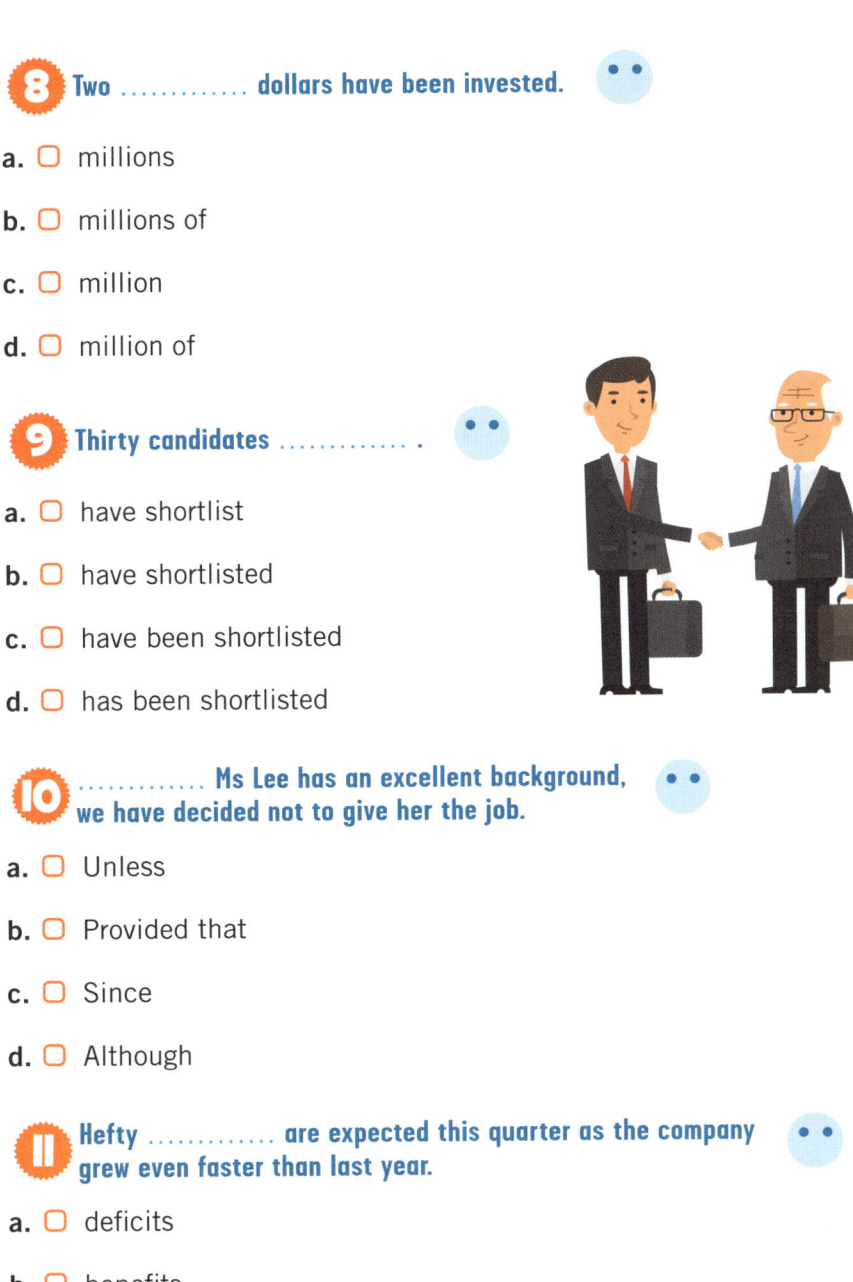

10 .... Ms Lee has an excellent background, we have decided not to give her the job.

a. ☐ Unless

b. ☐ Provided that

c. ☐ Since

d. ☐ Although

11 Hefty .... are expected this quarter as the company grew even faster than last year.

a. ☐ deficits

b. ☐ benefits

c. ☐ profits

d. ☐ debits

→ Voir réponses page 49.

PART 5 / EN CONDITIONS D'EXAMEN

12 **The director asked .... during the meeting.**

a. ☐ not to disturb

b. ☐ not to be disturbed

c. ☐ not disturbing

d. ☐ don't disturb

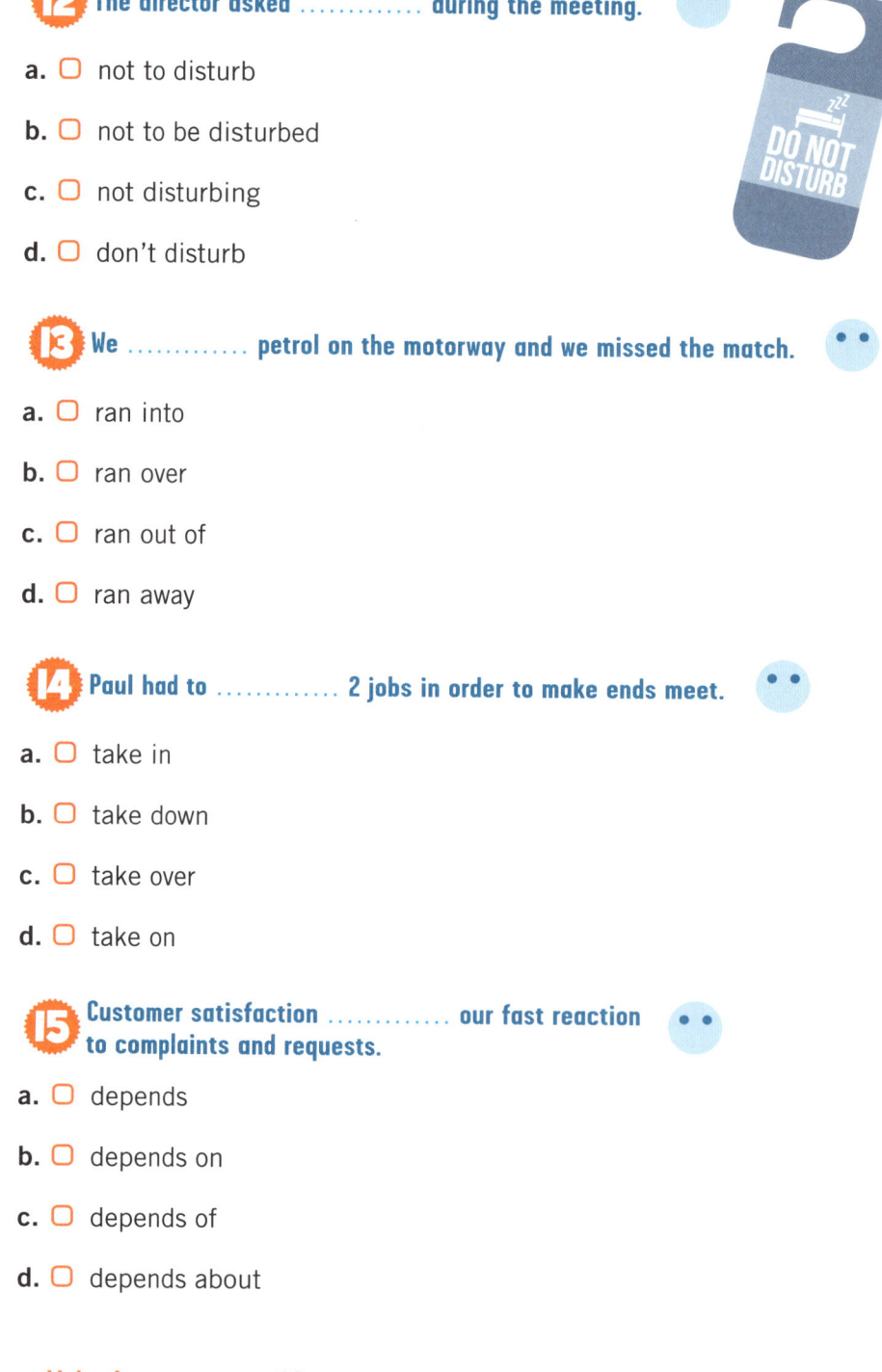

13 **We .... petrol on the motorway and we missed the match.**

a. ☐ ran into

b. ☐ ran over

c. ☐ ran out of

d. ☐ ran away

14 **Paul had to .... 2 jobs in order to make ends meet.**

a. ☐ take in

b. ☐ take down

c. ☐ take over

d. ☐ take on

15 **Customer satisfaction .... our fast reaction to complaints and requests.**

a. ☐ depends

b. ☐ depends on

c. ☐ depends of

d. ☐ depends about

→ **Voir réponses page 49.**

PART 5 / EN CONDITIONS D'EXAMEN

16 The incumbent chairman is .... the former one.

a. ☐ efficient than

b. ☐ far more efficient as

c. ☐ as efficient

d. ☐ far more efficient than

17 If you are .... applying for this position, you should fill in your application on line.

a. ☐ interested

b. ☐ interesting

c. ☐ interested in

d. ☐ interest in

18 She has worked hard .... her life and she now deserves a well-earned retirement.

a. ☐ long

b. ☐ while

c. ☐ through

d. ☐ throughout

19 I am .... seeking a job.

a. ☐ actually

b. ☐ actual

c. ☐ currently

d. ☐ now

→ Voir réponses page 49.

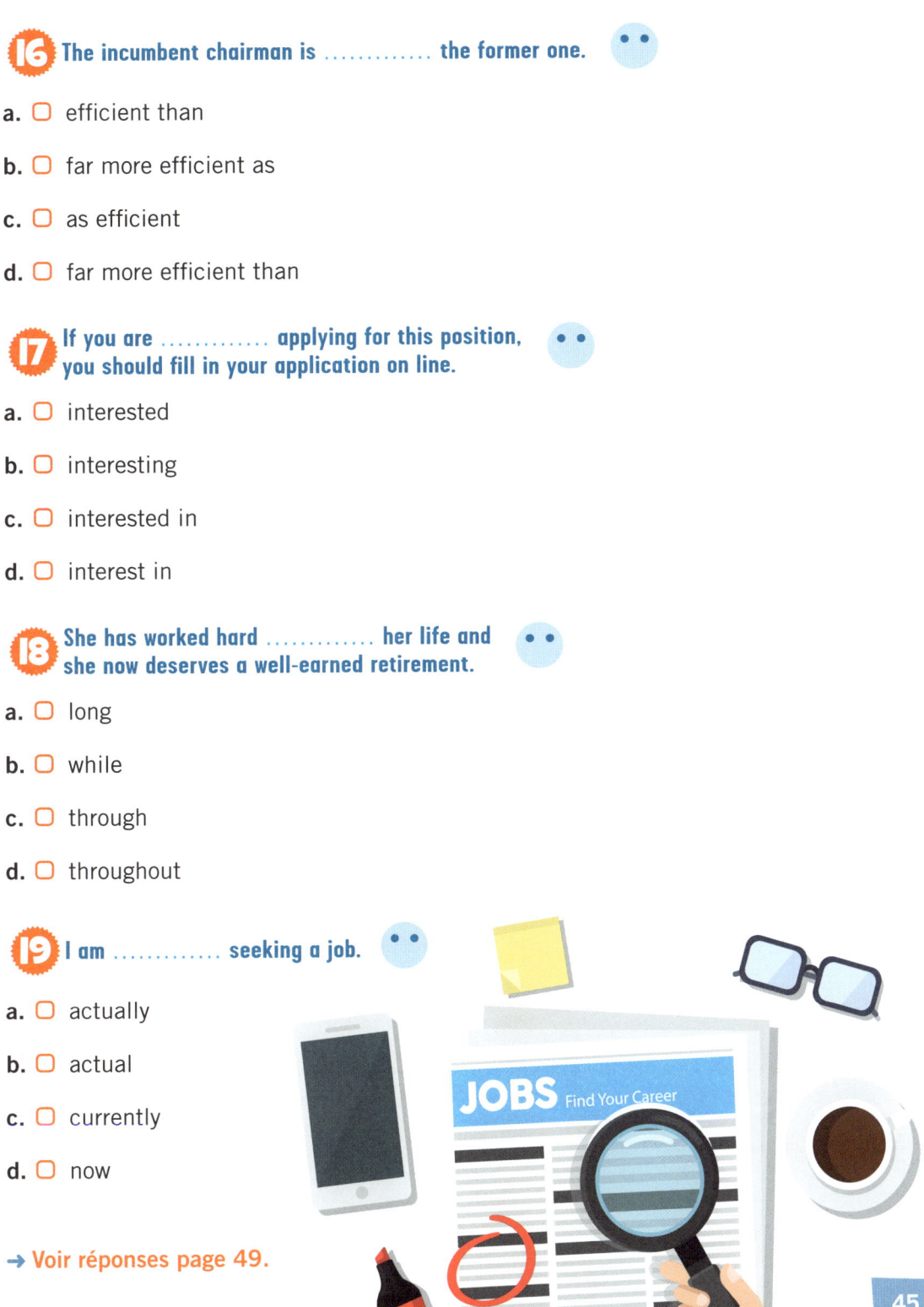

PART 5 / EN CONDITIONS D'EXAMEN

20. Only through .... policy will the firm make a profit.

a. ☐ consistent

b. ☐ consistently

c. ☐ consistence

d. ☐ constantly

21. Our business ....! That's awesome!

a. ☐ is thriving

b. ☐ is declining

c. ☐ is striving

d. ☐ is sinking

22. We'll have to offer more incentives to bolster this slow and .... market.

a. ☐ dynamic

b. ☐ sluggish

c. ☐ thriving

d. ☐ bustling

23. Prices dramatically .... so I can't afford these holidays anymore.

a. ☐ plummeted

b. ☐ soared

c. ☐ dropped

d. ☐ fell

→ **Voir réponses page 49.**

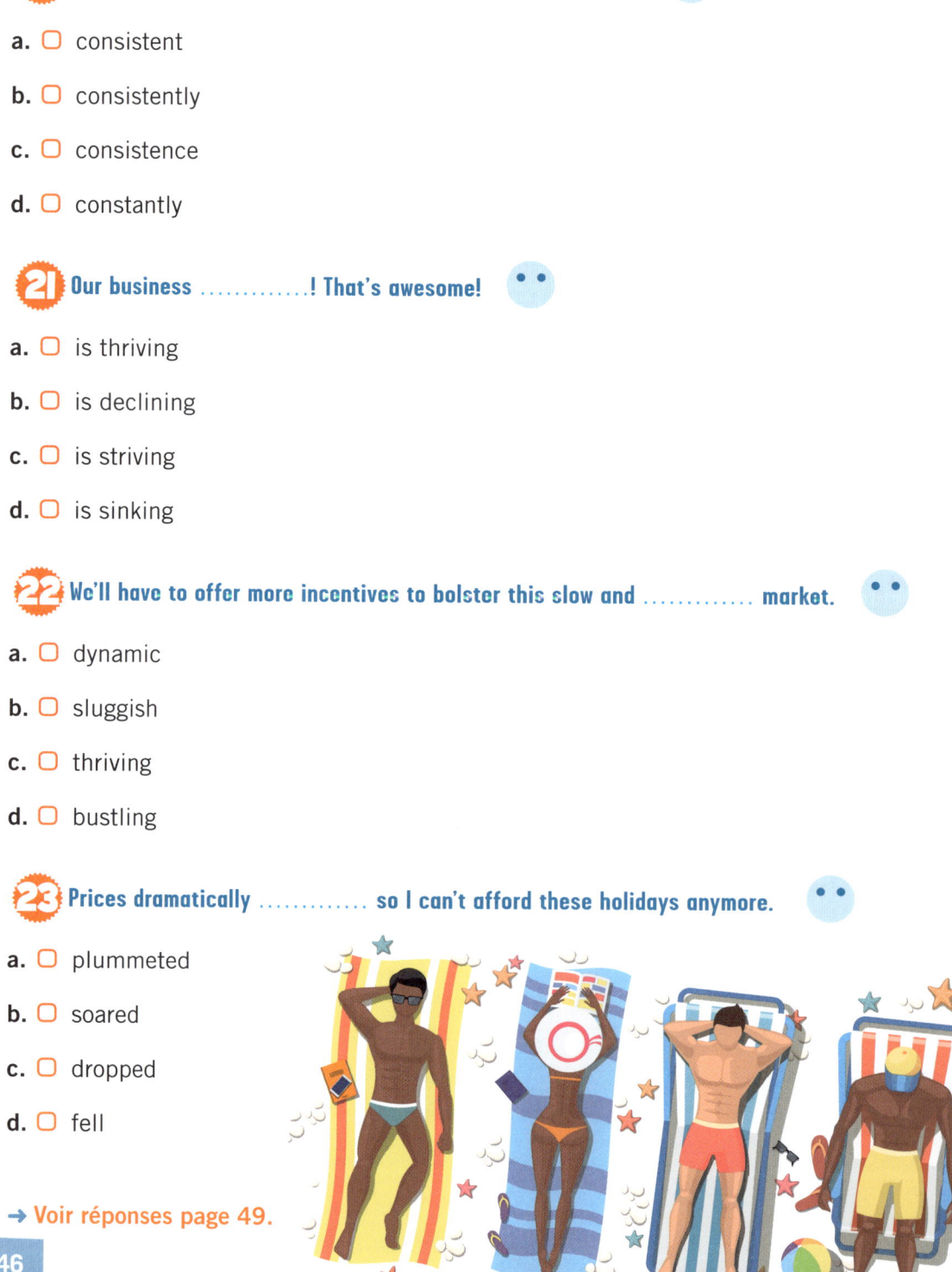

24 We were .... a mortgage. What a relief!

a. ☐ accepted

b. ☐ denied

c. ☐ granted

d. ☐ refused

25 Paul .... working with this team, he will have to adjust.

a. ☐ is not used to

b. ☐ uses to

c. ☐ is used

d. ☐ is used to

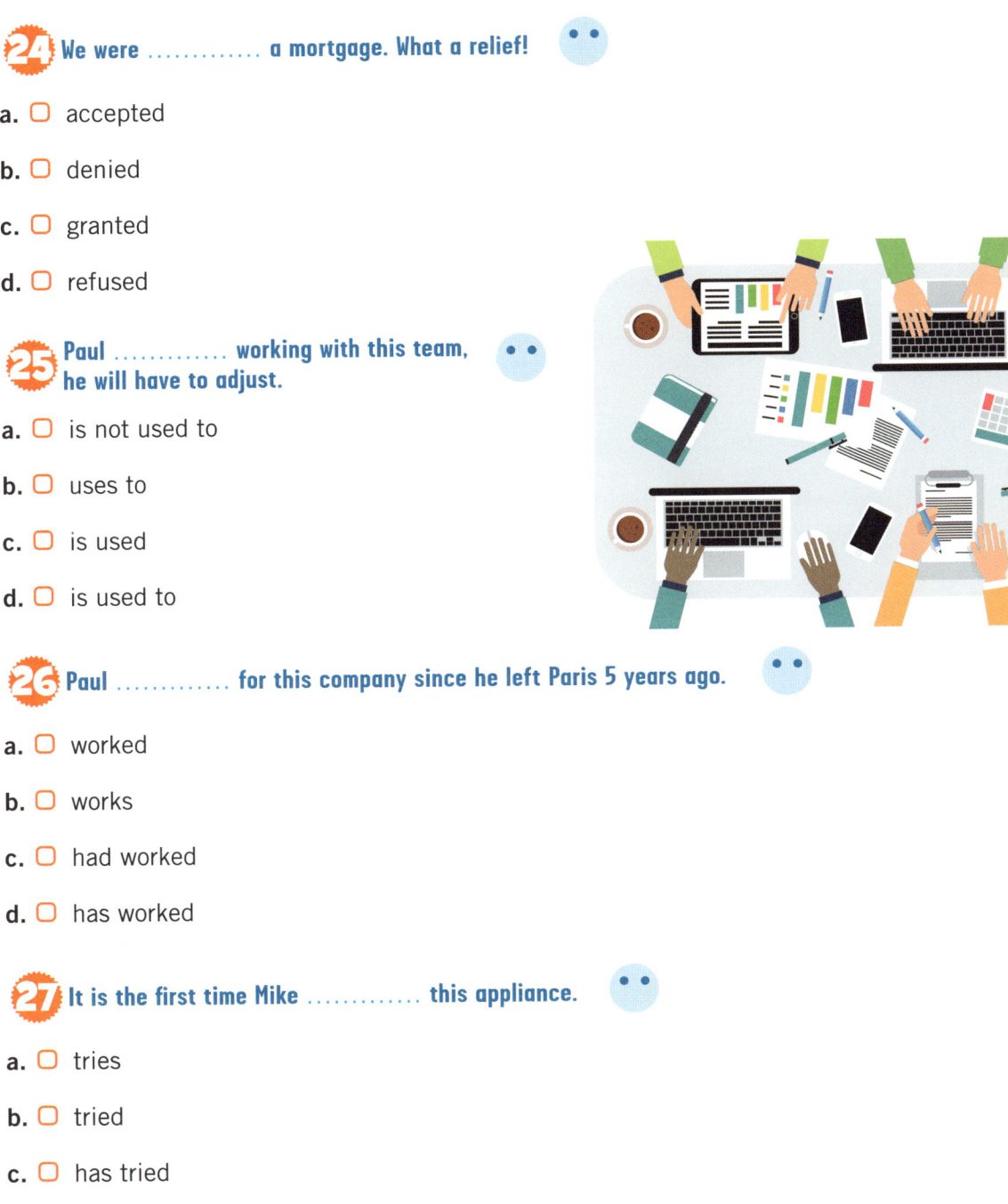

26 Paul .... for this company since he left Paris 5 years ago.

a. ☐ worked

b. ☐ works

c. ☐ had worked

d. ☐ has worked

27 It is the first time Mike .... this appliance.

a. ☐ tries

b. ☐ tried

c. ☐ has tried

d. ☐ is trying

→ Voir réponses page 49.

PART 5 / EN CONDITIONS D'EXAMEN

28 By the end of next year, the commission experts .... their conclusion.

a. ☐ will have produced

b. ☐ will produce

c. ☐ is producing

d. ☐ produces

29 It's high time we .... our expenses.

a. ☐ reduce

b. ☐ reduced

c. ☐ have reduced

d. ☐ are reducing

30 If I .... you, I wouldn't bid for it.

a. ☐ was

b. ☐ am

c. ☐ were

d. ☐ had been you

→ Voir réponses page 49.

Réponses
de ce test blanc n° 2

1 d.
2 b.
3 b.
4 a.
5 c.
6 a.
7 b.
8 c.
9 c.
10 d.

11 c.
12 b.
13 c.
14 d.
15 b.
16 d.
17 c.
18 d.
19 c.
20 a.

21 a.
22 b.
23 b.
24 c.
25 a.
26 d.
27 c.
28 a.
29 b.
30 c.

La partie 6 est très similaire à la partie 5. On y retrouve de nombreux points de grammaire, de conjugaison et de vocabulaire.

Les documents-supports peuvent être des lettres de correspondance, des e-mails, des mémos ou encore des articles. Il vous faudra compléter des phrases à l'intérieur d'un texte.

Cette partie vous propose 4 textes et 4 questions en Q.C.M.. Il vous faudra donc répondre à 16 questions en tout. Ne consacrez pas plus de 15 minutes à cette partie. C'est amplement suffisant si l'on a de la méthode et de l'entraînement.

La façon de procéder est simple : ne lisez pas le texte du début à la fin !

Lisez seulement la phrase à trou. Deux fois sur trois, vous trouverez directement la bonne réponse. Sinon lisez la phrase qui précède ou celle qui suit.

Part 6
Complete the text

Consigne

Application immédiate avec l'exercice qui suit, qui compose un texte complet mais qui a été segmenté en trois pour apporter la preuve que l'on peut trouver la réponse sans se préoccuper du contexte.

Training

Document 1

To: Lucy Nedlec
From: John Ash Accounts manager
Subject: change in fares
Date: September 3rd

Please find enclosed your invoice for your ambulance ride from June to August. Please note and be reminded that our fares ………….. This increase took effect on July 1st and is applied on the enclosed invoice.

a. ☐ are increasing

b. ☐ increase

c. ☐ will increase

d. ☐ have increased

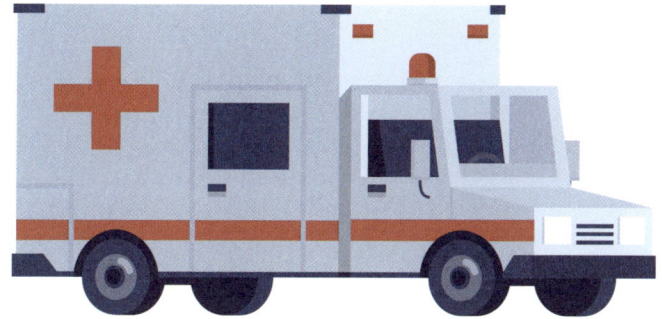

→ **Voir réponses page 64.**

PART 6 / TRAINING

All payments must be made payable to Ambulance Ride Services on the indicated due time. Please make sure you mail your payment at least 5 days before the maturity date. If you failed to meet the payment, you would be .... 5% on your next invoice.

a. ☐ charge

b. ☐ account

c. ☐ charged

d. ☐ ask

Thank you for riding and trusting Ambulance Ride Services. We are eager to provide fast, ... service that takes you safely wherever you need to go.

a. ☐ reliable

b. ☐ reliability

c. ☐ reliant

d. ☐ reliance

→ Voir réponses page 64.

PART 6 / TRAINING

4

Document 2

To: residents of Tromp Towers
From: Alexis Santos, property manager
Subject: facade cleaning
Date: July 1st

On July 15 our builders will begin renovating The Tromp Towers. They will be operating from Monday to Friday from 9:00 to 16:00. To ease their work, please remove every object which is on your windowsills or balconies .... July 15 and mind the fresh paint!

a. ☐ after   b. ☐ before   c. ☐ while   d. ☐ since

You should .... mind the ladders and scaffoldings which might block the access to the garages.

a. ☐ as well   b. ☐ too   c. ☐ also   d. ☐ never

Sorry for the inconvenience but the results will be .... it!

a. ☐ like   b. ☐ worth   c. ☐ worthy   d. ☐ trustworthy

➜ Voir réponses page 64.

PART 6 / TRAINING

7

Document 3

To: Xtra Employees<staff@xtra.com>

From: Joan Space<joan@xtra.com>

Date: October 15

Re: assistant manager

If you are interested in applying for the position of assistant manager, please contact me. I am the Human Ressources coordinator. I am in charge of the ………….

a. ☐ recruiter

b. ☐ recruitment

c. ☐ recruits

d. ☐ recruit

8

I will also present the position, explain the company policy and discuss the …………. compensation package.

a. ☐ year   b. ☐ annual   c. ☐ yearly   d. ☐ balance

➜ Voir réponses page 64.

You will be kept informed shortly after the deliberations if you have been ....

a. ☐ employ
b. ☐ engage
c. ☐ select
d. ☐ hired

Document 4

Dear Mr Sendral,

I have been an unwavering user of your cycling helmets since you launched the brand 15 years ago. But I am writing to you to ....

a. ☐ complain
b. ☐ complaint
c. ☐ discontent
d. ☐ dissatisfaction

→ **Voir réponses page 64.**

PART 6 / TRAINING

Indeed, I .... a new helmet last week and I used it immediately and after a ride I noticed a tiny crack on the side of the helmet.

a. ☐ am purchasing

b. ☐ purchase

c. ☐ purchased

d. ☐ have purchased

As I hadn't .... off or even let it drop, I reckon that the helmet is defective. I have enclosed the payment receipt and I hope you will send a replacement.

Thank you for taking my request into consideration.

Chris Nolah

a. ☐ fell

b. ☐ fall

c. ☐ fallen

d. ☐ felt

→ **Voir réponses page 64.**

PART 6 / TRAINING

Document 5

Dear Mr Nolah,
Thank you for riding with our helmets. Customer satisfaction is our priority. We are sorry to read that your item is defective. Please accept our ………….

a. ☐ excuse   b. ☐ apologizing   c. ☐ apologing   d. ☐ apologies

Be sure that everything will be …………. to satisfy your complaint.

a. ☐ make   b. ☐ repaired   c. ☐ implemented   d. ☐ fix

To thank you for your loyalty, in the package you will find a pair of cycling shorts from our new collection.

………….

Eric Sendral,
relationship manager

a. ☐ Yours faithfully   b. ☐ With love
c. ☐ My respect   d. ☐ Your faithfully

→ **Voir réponses page 64.**

59

LES TROIS PRÉSENTS

Le présent simple

Sa formation

Le présent simple est ainsi nommé car sa formation à la forme affirmative est simple : sujet + verbe.

Attention cependant aux 3e personnes du singulier : **il faut un « s »**.

Les choses se compliquent un peu avec les formes négatives et interrogatives car on doit faire intervenir un auxiliaire modal qui est :

Doesn't et **does** pour les 3e personnes du singulier et **don't** et **do** pour les autres personnes. Le verbe est alors **toujours** en **base verbale**.

Son emploi

On l'utilise pour les actions habituelles ou répétitives, pour ce qui est toujours vrai et pour les vérités générales.

Quelques mots-clés qui indiquent qu'il faut utiliser le présent simple : often, usually, sometimes, seldom, always.

Le présent en be + -ing

Sa formation

C'est un temps composé de l'auxiliaire **be** conjugué au présent + base verbale + **-ing**. Comme il y a déjà un auxiliaire, nul besoin d'en ajouter un autre. Pour la forme négative, il suffit de mettre **be** à la forme négative. Pour la forme interrogative, il faut inverser le sujet et le verbe « être ». Ce temps ne pose pas de problèmes particuliers aux Français. Nous l'utilisons souvent trop systématiquement.

Son emploi

On l'utilise pour les actions qui se déroulent au moment où l'on parle ou pour une action en cours. Il a aussi parfois une valeur de futur proche.

Quelques mots-clés qui indiquent qu'il faut utiliser le présent en be + -ing : look, listen, at the moment, now.

Le present perfect

Ce temps est mal maîtrisé car il n'a pas d'équivalent en français. Sa formation ressemble beaucoup au passé composé, mais gardez bien à l'esprit que le present perfect n'a aucun rapport avec un temps du passé. C'est un présent parfait qui permet de capturer l'instant.

Sa formation

Il est formé de l'auxiliaire **have** ou **has** + participe passé en **-ed** pour les verbes réguliers et 3ᵉ colonne du tableau (voir p. 112) pour les verbes irréguliers.

Son emploi

On l'utilise pour faire un constat ou un bilan ou pour faire le lien entre le passé et le présent.

Quelques mots-clés qui indiquent qu'il faut utiliser le present perfect : just, already, not yet, for, it is the first time, so far.

Le prétérit

Sa formation

Ce temps ressemble au présent simple. À la forme affirmative, il est formé de sujet + verbe en **-ed** pour les verbes réguliers et 2ᵉ colonne du tableau (voir p.112) des verbes irréguliers. Pour la forme négative, on utilise **didn't** et, pour la forme interrogative, on utilise **did**.

Son emploi

Il permet de traduire 3 temps du passé en français.

- **Passé composé** : *J'ai vu Paul hier*
    → I saw Paul yesterday.
- **Imparfait** : *Quand il habitait à Londres, il mangeait des fish & chips.*
    → When he lived in London he ate fish & chips.
- **Passé simple** : *Il la vit, la suivit et la tua.*
    → He saw her, followed her and killed her.

16 Conjuguez le verbe au temps qui convient : présent simple, présent en be + -ing, present perfect ou prétérit.

a. Look at you! You **(grow)** ....!

b. I **(lose)** .... the contract and had no choice but to do it again.

c. Can I have this book? No, it **(be reprint)** ....

d. .... you ever **(eat)** .... kangaroo meat?

e. He rarely **(communicate)** .... with his colleagues.

f. You **(drink)** .... too much! You can't drive.

g. What .... I **(do)** .... to deserve this?

→ Voir réponses page 65.

h. He was working when the news (break out) ....

i. I .... never (see) .... that man before.

j. The sales (skyrocket) .... since we advertised.

17 Entourez la bonne réponse.

a. The company's policy **changed / is changing / has changed**.
We can't do this anymore.

b. Hello! I **phone / am phoning / have phoned** to confirm a reservation.

c. We **hired / have hired / hire** three cashiers last month.

d. So far, 20 000 bottles **have been sold / were sold / sell** overseas.

e. We **don't see / didn't see / haven't seen** Paul for ages.

f. I can't believe it! You **forgot / are forgetting / have forgotten** your keys.

g. We will call you as soon as we **have arrived / arrive / are arriving**.

h. It is high time you **tell / told / have told** the truth.

i. Sorry! The manager **has just left / just left / just leave**.

j. We **received / have received / receive** your order today.

→ Voir réponses page 65.

Réponses
training

d. La réponse **a.** n'est pas correcte car les prix ne sont pas en train d'augmenter. La réponse **b.** n'est pas correcte, car le présent simple exprime une action habituelle et répétitive. La réponse **c.** n'est pas correcte, car les prix ont déjà augmenté, donc le futur est impossible. La réponse **d.** est correcte car le present perfect est le temps du constat et du bilan.

c. Il vous suffit juste d'identifier **would be**. Le seul choix possible est alors un participe passé. Réponse **c.**

a. Ici encore la seule réponse possible est la **a.**, car devant le nom **service** on ne peut mettre qu'un adjectif.

b.

c. Cette question est très facile ! Il y a parfois de grandes différences de difficulté entre les questions.

b. « because I am worth it! »

b.

c. Yearly = annual balance = *bilan*.

d. To be hired = to be employed = to get the job.

a.

c.

c. Apprenez bien les verbes irréguliers. Après l'auxiliaire **have**, il faut un participe passé.

d.

c.

15

a. Yours faithfully = best regards = yours sincerely = cordially.

a. have grown **b.** lost **c.** is being reprinted **d.** Have you ever eaten **e.** he rarely communicates **f.** have drunk **g.** did … do **h.** broke out **i.** I have … seen. **j.** have skyrocketed.

a. has changed **b.** am phoning **c.** hired **d.** have been sold **e.** haven't seen **f.** have forgotten **g.** arrive **h.** told **i.** has just left **j.** received.

Consigne

**Voici 4 textes et les 16 questions Q.C.M.
tels qu'ils vous seront présentés lors de la certification.**

PART 6 / EN CONDITIONS D'EXAMEN

En conditions d'examen

Text 1

To: James Lee

From: Jane Turner

Subject: Product launch

Hi James,

I am writing ❶...... the launching of the Dreemer product we discussed last week.

As you recall, we talked about the ❷...... placement of the product on the market.

❸...... my ❹...... suggestions.

Jane

❶

a. ☐ about it
b. ☐ because of
c. ☐ refer to
d. ☐ in reference to

❷

a. ☐ optimal
b. ☐ optimally
c. ☐ opt
d. ☐ option

❸

a. ☐ regarding
b. ☐ are attached
c. ☐ please find attached
d. ☐ attached

❹

a. ☐ later
b. ☐ late
c. ☐ latest
d. ☐ last

→ **Voir réponses page 71.**

67

PART 6 / EN CONDITIONS D'EXAMEN

Text 2

Switching to green power is rapidly becoming an ❺...... issue, as companies consider becoming more eco-friendly. ❻......, there is still a lot to do because businesses tend to focus on short term profit and dividend paid to shareholders.

The major issues of environmental sustainibility and energy transition ❼...... denied.

It is high time every company ❽...... a gear.

❺

a. ☐ economist
b. ☐ economy
c. ☐ economic
d. ☐ economical

❻

a. ☐ however
b. ☐ admittedly
c. ☐ because
d. ☐ logically

❼

a. ☐ not
b. ☐ cannot do
c. ☐ can never
d. ☐ can no longer be

❽

a. ☐ move up
b. ☐ moved up
c. ☐ is moving
d. ☐ must moving

➜ **Voir réponses page 71.**

Text 3

Have you got trouble ......? Tired of ...... tired? Then try Rythm Dream helmet. It claims to be the first active wearable to .... sleep quality. Can it work? It is ....

Then don't lose a minute and ask for a free trial.

a. ☐ to sleep
b. ☐ at sleep
c. ☐ sleep
d. ☐ sleeping

a. ☐ be
b. ☐ to be
c. ☐ being
d. ☐ not to be

a. ☐ lose
b. ☐ lessen
c. ☐ lower
d. ☐ improve

a. ☐ scientifically evidence
b. ☐ scientifically proven
c. ☐ scientifically proof
d. ☐ prooved

→ Voir réponses page 71.

PART 6 / EN CONDITIONS D'EXAMEN

Text 4

To: all staff

From: Bill Carter, President

Date: May 13, 2018

Subject: annual company picnic

The annual company picnic ...... at Memorial Park on July 13, 2018. This event ...... by Fresh Barbecue with desserts by Lucy's Sweet Things. Immediate family members ....

Please contact Susan Page to ....

a. ⬜ is held
b. ⬜ will be held
c. ⬜ held
d. ⬜ is holding

a. ⬜ will be catered
b. ⬜ will cater
c. ⬜ was catered
d. ⬜ cater

a. ⬜ will invite
b. ⬜ is invited
c. ⬜ are invited
d. ⬜ invite

a. ⬜ enroll
b. ⬜ register
c. ⬜ enter
d. ⬜ sign up

➔ **Voir réponses page 71.**

Réponses
de cette mise en conditions

1 d.
2 a.
3 c.
4 c.
5 c.
6 a.
7 d.
8 b.
9 d.
10 c.
11 d.
12 b.
13 b.
14 a.
15 c.
16 d.

Cette partie comporte 54 questions :
- 29 questions portant sur 10 documents uniques,
- 25 questions portant sur environ 12 ensembles de 2 ou 3 textes ou documents.
Les textes sont des e-mails, des lettres, des mémos, des brochures ou des graphiques.
<u>Attention, en aucun cas vous n'aurez le temps de lire les textes de A à Z et encore moins de les traduire !</u>

Part 7
Comprehension

Training

Optimiser sa lecture

Bien qu'il soit recommandé de ne pas lire les textes dans leur intégralité, il va néanmoins falloir les parcourir.

La lecture mobilise la vue et deux types de mémoires (visuelle et sémantique).

Quand on lit, l'œil voit les mots, puis les envoie au cerveau qui les transforme en images et les compare ensuite à ce qu'il connaît : c'est la **mémoire visuelle**.

Dans un deuxième temps, on met un sens sur ces mots, ce qui nous permet de comprendre la phrase : c'est la **mémoire sémantique**.

Ces deux processus se font rapidement et automatiquement, mais, en ce qui concerne l'anglais, les choses se compliquent, car c'est une langue étrangère… Bonne nouvelle néanmoins, les phrases du TOEIC® ne sont pas alambiquées et sont souvent construites sur ce modèle : sujet + verbe + complément.

Pour devenir un **lecteur rapide**, il est recommandé de repérer les **mots-cibles**, d'abord dans les questions, puis vous ferez appel à votre vision périphérique pour retrouver ce mot dans le texte.

Pour être encore plus efficace, **cherchez le mot dans le texte** en suivant les lignes avec un stylo qui vous servira de guide visuel et qui empêchera l'œil de revenir en arrière ou de saccader votre lecture…

Il faut donc **commencer par lire les questions**, puis aller repérer les informations concordantes dans le texte, ensuite, lire les propositions de réponses et, enfin, répondre.

Il faudra parfois faire de petits calculs intermédiaires (addition, soustraction et multiplication simples), car la réponse ne se trouvera pas telle quelle dans le texte. Attention, on continue d'essayer de vous piéger : ne vous « jetez » pas sur les chiffres ou les mots dès qu'ils apparaissent.

Pour résumer :
- Commencez par lire les questions qui se trouvent après le texte.
- Repérez les informations concordantes dans le texte.
- Lisez les réponses.
- Répondez.

PART 7 / TRAINING

Document 1

NOTICE OF MEETING OF SHAREHOLDERS OF SHALE OIL CY.

Dear shareholders,

Please find with the hereby given that the annual meeting of shareholders of Shale cy will be held

**at 354 East St, Houston, Texas, USA
on September 3rd at 15:00.**

The agenda will focus on :

1. re-election of Bruce Pepper as CEO.

2. approval of the final dividend.

3. shareholder issues.

4. amendments of the statutes to limit the merger and acquisitions without special approval.

If you are unable to attend this meeting, you will be requested to execute and mail the enclosed form of proxy.

1 How often do shareholders meet?

a. ☐ Once a week.

b. ☐ Once a month.

c. ☐ Twice a year.

d. ☐ Once a year.

2 Which topic agenda will be addressed?

a. ☐ The turnover.

b. ☐ Amending the constitution.

c. ☐ Reappoint the existing CEO.

d. ☐ Income redistribution.

Conseil
Notez que, à ce stade, vous n'avez pas lu le texte dans sa totalité…

3 What will the shareholders who cannot attend the meeting have to do?

a. ☐ Wait for next year.

b. ☐ Get an authorized substitute.

c. ☐ Vote online.

d. ☐ Execute the secretary.

→ **Voir réponses page 86.**

PART 7 / TRAINING

Document 2

Conseil

Avec ce document, pas de texte, juste un tableau. **As easy as pie!** Un jeu d'enfant ! Regardez les questions, puis cherchez la réponse dans le texte. Vous devez mettre moins de 2 minutes pour faire cet exercice.

DEPARTURE	ARRIVAL	DESTINATION	FLIGHT	EXPECTED DELAY	CONDITIONS
08:00	13:00	LONDON	N472	40 MINUTES	FOG
09:30	12:00	COPENHAGEN	1917	50 MINUTES	HAIL
13:00	15:00	BERLIN	K140	20 MINUTES	RAIN
13:08	13:48	HONG KONG	KS91	CANCELLED	
14:02	14:02	ROME	R569	ON TIME	
14:18	14:18	MADRID	D313	CANCELLED	
14:24	14:24	SYDNEY	Y560	DELAYED	
16:00	18:00	BARCELONA	Y800	ON TIME	CLEAR

4 What time does the flight to London usually leave?

a. ☐ 8 pm

b. ☐ 1 pm

c. ☐ 8 am

d. ☐ 1 am

5 Why is the flight to Copenhagen delayed?

a. ☐ It's snowing.

b. ☐ It's stormy.

c. ☐ It's misty.

d. ☐ It's icy.

6 What time should the passengers have landed in Denmark?

a. ☐ midday

b. ☐ 13:00

c. ☐ 9:30 am

d. ☐ 1 pm

→ **Voir réponses page 86.**

PART 7 / TRAINING

Conseil

On continue, prenez confiance en vous ! Le texte est toujours aussi court, on applique la même méthode : on va directement aux questions puis on va « à la pêche » aux réponses dans le texte.

Document 3

Help needed

Are you a college student? You find it difficult to make ends meet? Here is an opportunity to make an extra money by working at SPOON the best dinning hall on campus.

Hours

Part-time job, 25 hours per week, $350 per week.

Job description

Application opened to all freshmen students provided they are over 18. Appropriate clothing must be worn. Possibility to choose working times.

Please apply online at : spoon.boston@campus.com

PART 7 / TRAINING

7 Who is this ad addressed to?

a. ☐ All students.

b. ☐ Underage students.

c. ☐ Undergraduate students.

d. ☐ Waiters.

8 How much is the monthly salary?

a. ☐ $350

b. ☐ $700

c. ☐ $1,050

d. ☐ $1,400

9 Which statement is not true?

a. ☐ Unexperienced students are accepted.

b. ☐ Overage students are welcome.

c. ☐ Smart appearance needed.

d. ☐ Possibilty to work nightshift.

→ **Voir réponses pages 86-87.**

PART 7 / TRAINING

Conseil

Le texte de ce document est plus dense que celui des précédents. Pas de panique : lors de la certification, les textes sont très bien structurés et les informations sont présentées point par point. Lisez les questions, repérez les informations dans le texte et n'oubliez pas qu'il y a des pièges !

Document 4

CRIME & THRILLER BOOK CLUB

JOIN OUR CLUB AND:

- get access to our selection of the world's best detective stories, crime and thriller books and mystery novels.
- join us in a click by visiting our website
- save up to 48% off publishers' edition prices all year.

Join us now!

Enroll online in a few minutes and let yourself be guided.

1 Select your type of book by clicking on 'add to cart' for each title you want to order. Your book is now in your shopping cart but it can be removed by clicking on 'remove' if you have a second thought.

2 Fill out the enrollment form. Provide your name and address for shipment.

3 Accept the conditions and agree to the membership.

4 Provide your payment information.

5 Review and confirm your order by checking your shopping cart. Check if the promotion code has been applied and then click 'continue' to pay.

Congratulations on your enrollment, welcome to our club!

GET 6 BOOKS FOR $48!

PART 7 / TRAINING

10 Which of the following is not an advantage of joining Crime & Thriller Book Club?

a. ☐ You can have books at discount prices.

b. ☐ You can read the world's greatest detective fiction.

c. ☐ You can buy all books.

d. ☐ Enrollment is quick.

11 Which statement is not correct?

a. ☐ You'll become a member if you buy books.

b. ☐ You can buy romantic novels.

c. ☐ You will get discounts.

d. ☐ You can change your mind.

12 What is not true?

a. ☐ The customer can't add anything in his shopping cart.

b. ☐ The customer can use his promotion code.

c. ☐ The customer must provide his credit card number.

d. ☐ The customer must give his address.

→ **Voir réponses page 87.**

PART 7 / TRAINING

Document 5

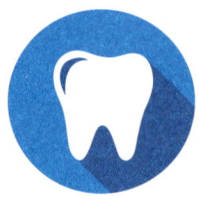

DIY DENTAL KITS

Would you superglue a chipped tooth? According to a survey conducted by the Chicago dental Society 70% of dentists reported that they've seen patients who try to fix their dental problems on their own before going to their dentists.

Most of the time people buy kits from their local supermarkets. These kits come with instruments dentists use and you can repair fillings, pull out teeth, fix chipped teeth and dentures.

People think that doing it themselves will save them money (the kit costs $5.5) but actually it can cause costly damage to your teeth and may put your health at risk if you get an infection.

PART 7 / TRAINING

13 **What is the article about?**

a. ☐ Toothpaste.

b. ☐ Dentists.

c. ☐ Tooth repair.

d. ☐ DIY shops.

14 **Why do so many people use DIY dental kits?**

a. ☐ Because it's safe.

b. ☐ Because it is cheaper.

c. ☐ Because it's fun.

d. ☐ Because they want to become dentists.

15 **What can't you do with a dental kit?**

a. ☐ Make an anaesthesia.

b. ☐ Repair a filling.

c. ☐ Use instruments.

d. ☐ Pull out a tooth.

→ **Voir réponses page 87.**

PART 7 / TRAINING / RÉPONSES

Réponses
training

d. Sans même regarder le texte ou les réponses vous le devinez, non ? Allez vérifier dans le texte. **Annual** vous indique que c'est la réponse **d.**

c. Cherchez le mot-clé **CEO** dans le texte. **Re elect** ➡ **re appoint**.

b. Les questions suivent (souvent) l'ordre du texte, cherchez donc dans le dernier paragraphe. Bien sûr, si on sait que **by proxy** veut dire « procuration », cela aide un tantinet… Apprenez ce mot par cœur !

a. am ➡ avant midi ; **pm** ➡ passé midi.

d. hail = grêle **(ice)**.

a. Il faut connaître un peu sa géographie, les pays et les capitales. **Land** ➡ atterrir ; **take off** ➡ décoller. **Midday** ➡ **noon** ➡ **12:00**. Copenhagen, capital of Denmark.

c. Pour cette question, il faut un peu de culture. Au **college** (université, aux USA), on est **undergraduate** c'est-à-dire que l'on n'a pas encore la licence. Les étudiants de 1re année sont des **freshmen** (même si l'on est une femme), ceux de 2e année des **sophomores** et des **seniors**, l'année de la licence. **Underage** ➡ **under 18**.

PART 7 / TRAINING / RÉPONSES

d. Voilà un peu de calcul : $350 x 4 (semaines) = $1,400. Attention, vous n'avez pas droit à la calculette, ni au téléphone.

a. La **a.** est la bonne réponse car aucune mention n'est faite sur l'expérience professionnelle. Cette question peut vous apparaître un peu plus complexe, mais pensez à mobiliser toute votre culture anglo-saxonne. Travaillez aussi le vocabulaire avec les synonymes et les antonymes. **Underage** est le contraire de **overage** ; **freshman** = **1st year at college**.

c. Dans le texte, il est dit **a selection of**.

b. Attention à ces questions qui comportent des **not**, car elles nécessitent une petite gymnastique intellectuelle.

a.

c.

b.

a.

Consigne

Nous vous proposons ici une série de documents et des questions en Q.C.M.. Pour rappel, lors de la certification, vous seront posées 54 questions :

- 29 questions portant sur 10 documents uniques,
- 25 questions portant sur environ 12 ensembles de 2 ou 3 textes ou documents.

PART 7 / EN CONDITIONS D'EXAMEN

En conditions d'examen

40% OFF
Pizza and side orders over £40 at PIZZA HOT delivery.

Terms & conditions:

→ Valid on delivery, cannot be used in restaurant.

→ Excludes dips, drinks and dessert.

→ Cannot be used in conjunction with any other offer or deal.

→ Offers may vary by location. Check with local brand.

→ Valid through May 31.

PART 7 / EN CONDITIONS D'EXAMEN

1 What is not true?

a. ☐ You have to spend at least £40.

b. ☐ You can combine with other coupon.

c. ☐ The discount applies on salad.

d. ☐ Not all brands offer this deal.

2 What is true?

a. ☐ All restaurants offer this deal.

b. ☐ It's only valid from the 1st of June.

c. ☐ The rebate applies on pizza and salad.

d. ☐ You can only order online.

→ **Voir réponses page 109.**

MEMO TO CO WORKERS

To: all staff and interns

From: Lucy Lee Executive Assistant to the President

Date: July 13

Subject: dishes in the sink

It has come to our attention that there has been a pile of unwashed dishes that accumulates in the sink by the end of each week. It has got so bad that washing one's hand in the kitchen sink becomes an uncomfortable undertaking.

Therefore, we are introducing a new policy that mandates that employees wash their dishes as soon as they are done with them, keeping the sink clear for other uses.

If you don't have the time to wash your lunch containers or coffee mug, leave it by your desk until you are ready to wash it. Even two or three dirty plates will encourage every person thereafter to leave their unwashed food-stained and silverware in the sink. Conversely, studies have shown that when a sink is empty, people are more likely to wash their dishes immediately.

Thanks for your cooperation.

Best,

Lucy Lee

PART 7 / EN CONDITIONS D'EXAMEN

3. Who will read this memorandum?

a. ☐ The cleaning staff.

b. ☐ All employees.

c. ☐ Visitors.

d. ☐ Clients.

4. What is the issue of the memo?

a. ☐ People are dirty.

b. ☐ People eat too much.

c. ☐ People are overwhelmed with work.

d. ☐ People don't do the washing up.

5. What must all staff do?

a. ☐ Eat at their desk.

b. ☐ Use disposable dishes.

c. ☐ Wash their containers systematically.

d. ☐ Bring their dishes home.

→ **Voir réponses page 109.**

Having a problem with a product or a service can be frustrating. When you are trying to resolve a problem with a company, the first step should be to discuss your concerns with a representative of the business. If a phone call or email doesn't resolve the problem consider writing a complaint letter.

A letter is important: it puts your complaint on a record with the company, helps preserve any legal rights you may have in the situation and lets the company know you're serious about pursuing the complaint.

Use these tips to write an effective complaint:

➡ **Be clear and concise**. Describe the item or service you bought and the problem. Include serial or model numbers and the name and location of the seller.

➡ **State exactly what you want done** and how long you're willing to wait for a response. Be reasonable.

➡ **Don't write an angry, sarcastic or threatening letter** as the person reading is not responsible for the problem.

➡ **Include copies of relevant documents like receipts,** work orders and warranties.

➡ **Send your letter by certified mail** and request a return receipt.

PART 7 / EN CONDITIONS D'EXAMEN

6 Why write a letter?

a. ☐ To show you have nice handwriting.

b. ☐ Because it is more effective.

c. ☐ Because it is faster than an email.

d. ☐ Because it is a legal record.

7 An effective letter should be…

a. ☐ aggressive.

b. ☐ in a breezy style.

c. ☐ respectful.

d. ☐ ironical.

8 What kind of letter should it be?

a. ☐ A standard letter.

b. ☐ With a return receipt.

c. ☐ With a postcard.

d. ☐ A registered letter with no acknowledgement of delivery.

→ **Voir réponses page 109.**

Conseil

Lisez les deux textes qui sont mis en relation. La méthode reste la même : prenez d'abord connaissance des réponses !

FISH & CHEAP RESTAURANT
54 Bracken Place
Southampton SO 16 3RB
tel (0141) 568 4305

PURCHASE ORDER

Vendor
MOBY DICK suppliers
45 Starfish road
Cornwall PL27
Tel (0141) 785 3891

Ship to:
Scarlett Santo
Restaurant manager
Address above

Ref: N°541
Date: January 15, 2018

Invoice to:
Sam Smith
Accountant
Address above

Order prepared by Joan Gold
Delivery date: January, 18, 2018

Items	Quantity	Unit cost	Total cost
Squid	300 pounds	£5	£1,500
Oyster	120 pounds	£3	£360
Scallop	350 pounds	£7	£2,450
Prawn	300 pounds	£2.50	£750
			sub total: £5,060
			shipping 5%: £253
			total: £5,313

Scarlett Santo
Restaurant manager
Fish & Cheap restaurant
54 Bracken place
Southampton So16 3RB

Dear Ms Santo,

Thank you for the purchase order that you e-mailed me. Unfortunately, we won't be able to meet the delivery date. Indeed the period is too short and we normally need 10 days to fill it. If you insist on keeping the original delivery date we will have to charge you an extra £150.

Moreover, because of bad weather conditions, the fishermen couldn't get out to fish. That's why we won't be able to provide you as many prawns as you ordered. Only 100 pounds. However we could replace them by frozen shrimps. The cost would be £300 for 200 pounds.

To summarize, your new total amount comes to £5,253.

Please call or e-mail me asap.
Best regards
Joan Gold

PART 7 / EN CONDITIONS D'EXAMEN

9 When is the order due?

a. ☐ January 15.

b. ☐ January 25.

c. ☐ 10 days after the order.

d. ☐ January 18.

10 Why won't the order be fulfilled?

a. ☐ The weather is too hot.

b. ☐ There is a fish shortage.

c. ☐ There are plenty of fish in the sea.

d. ☐ The fishermen overfished.

11 How much is the shipping fee after the extra charge?

a. ☐ £150.

b. ☐ £253.

c. ☐ 5%.

d. ☐ £403.

➜ Voir réponses page 109.

PART 7 / EN CONDITIONS D'EXAMEN

Conseil
Les deux documents suivants servent de supports aux questions qui suivent.

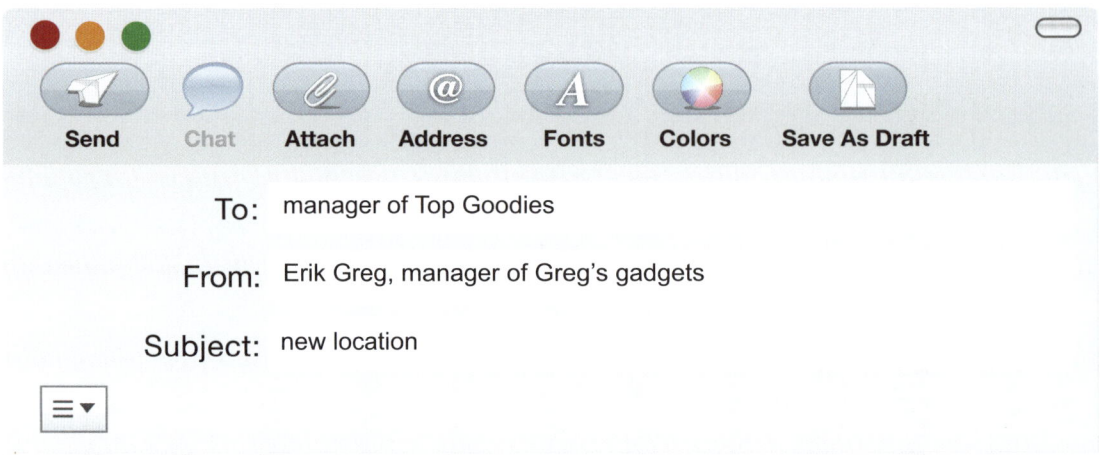

Date: 15, June 2018

Dear Paul Handy,

Here at Greg's gadgets were are very excited to merge and to have you all on board to embark on this new adventure. We have long admired the craftsmanship put into everyone and we are longing to become one big family.
Since we are going to outgrow our current locations (from 117 employees to 253) I wanted to give you an update on our search for an office big enough to house our teams.
We have found a beautiful location and we are close to signing a lease.
The new building is at 730 Lincoln Ave downtown. It is ideally located. It is close to shops and restaurants. It is only one block from the train station and half a mile from a car-free bike path. Great for all commuters.
You will please find attached an extract from the lease. I am convinced that the premises are perfect to shelter our business. I will sign the commercial lease as soon as I get your feedback.

I look forward to hearing from you.
Erik Greg

File attached: commercial lease agreement

The lease agreement is made to and entered on August 1 2018 by and between Top Goodies (hereafter referred as to Tenant) and Temple CB (hereafter referred as Landlord).

Article 1: Lease term

The term of this lease shall begin on the Commencement Date August 1 2018 and shall terminate on August 2023 provided however that at the option of the Tenant, Tenant may renew this lease for 5 additional successive one – year terms at a monthly rent of $25,000 per month, provide that notice of such renewal is given in writing no less than 120 days prior to the termination date.

Tenant may at any time cancel this lease and terminate all of its obligations hereunder by the payment of $75,000.

PART 7 / EN CONDITIONS D'EXAMEN

12 What will happen between Top Goodies and Greg's Gadgets?

a. ☐ They will get married.

b. ☐ Top Goodies will take control of Greg's gadgets.

c. ☐ They will merge.

d. ☐ They will split.

13 What is the lease term?

a. ☐ A month.

b. ☐ A year.

c. ☐ A year renewable.

d. ☐ 5 years.

14 What will be the charge if the Tenant wants to end the lease?

a. ☐ 3 times the amount of the lease.

b. ☐ $25,000.

c. ☐ No charge.

d. ☐ $120.

15 Why shouldn't Erik Greg miss the opportunity to rent the premises?

a. ☐ Because it is not a high rent.

b. ☐ Because it is close to facilities.

c. ☐ Because Paul Handy agrees.

d. ☐ Because it is located in a rural area.

→ **Voir réponses page 109.**

PART 7 / EN CONDITIONS D'EXAMEN

Conseil
Les trois documents suivants servent de supports aux questions qui suivent.

Document 1

XY company needs to focus advertising on Internet sites that appeal to young people. According to surveys, 72% of our target markets uses the internet more than 3 hours per week. The following list shows the most frequented sites in order of popularity:

> Toogle

> Head Book

> Your Space

Shifting our efforts from our media sources such as radio and magazine to these popular Internet sites will effectively promote our product sales. Young adults are spending more and more time on the Internet downloading music, communicating and less and less time reading magazines or listening to the radio. As the trend for cultural icons go to digital so must our marketing plans.

PART 7 / EN CONDITIONS D'EXAMEN

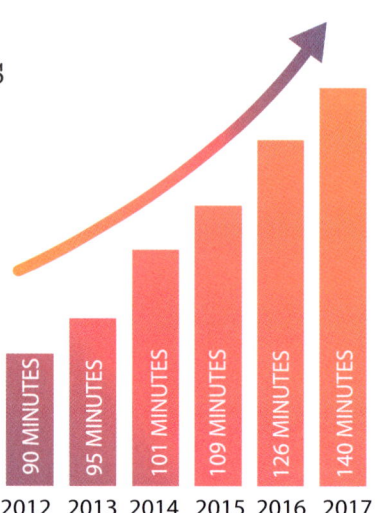

DAILY TIME SPENT ON SOCIAL NETWORKING BY INTERNET USERS WORLDWIDE FROM 2012 TO 2017 IN MINUTES.

90 MINUTES — 2012
95 MINUTES — 2013
101 MINUTES — 2014
109 MINUTES — 2015
126 MINUTES — 2016
140 MINUTES — 2017

In a world where people are spending more and more time watching streaming and consuming media more than ever, traditional TV is still king. But the gap is closing fast.

In 2016, people spent an average of 170 minutes of TV viewing per day. But the Internet wasn't too far behind with an average of 140 minutes per day.

Data also reveals that in the USA 60% of social media time was spent via smartphone App.

PART 7 / EN CONDITIONS D'EXAMEN

16 What is not true?

a. ☐ Companies favor the Internet to advertise.

b. ☐ TV viewing is leading by far.

c. ☐ The Internet is gaining ground.

d. ☐ People spent 140 minutes per day on the net in 2017.

17 What is no longer trendy?

a. ☐ Streaming.

b. ☐ Downloading music.

c. ☐ Connecting to the Internet with a computer.

d. ☐ Using Apps.

18 How long did people spend per day on the Net in 2012?

a. ☐ Less than an hour.

b. ☐ An hour.

c. ☐ 2 hours.

d. ☐ An hour and a half.

19 What can be inferred?

a. ☐ The Internet will lose its popularity.

b. ☐ Traditional media will disappear.

c. ☐ The use of the Internet will remain stable.

d. ☐ Head Book will go bust.

→ **Voir réponses page 109.**

PART 7 / EN CONDITIONS D'EXAMEN

"Sorry Rockies, we are skiing somewhere else!"

CLUB ALPINE

ALL-INCLUSIVE SKI EXPERIENCES.

Out here in the Alps, the all-inclusive offer is really all it takes to make the ultimate ski vacation. After all, with ski passes to the world's best ski domains, ski lessons with French Ski School, authentic and locally sourced cuisine and the rest you'd naturally expect from all-inclusive vacation. The choice is obvious.

What is included in your ski vacation?

- Lift tickets & group lessons
- Children clubs for ages 4-17
- All day gourmet dining & open bar (only soft drinks)
- After ski activities and entertainment for all
- Free Wi-Fi

Winter wonderlands!

Take on the downhill of VAL THO, a must for winter sports enthusiasts with majestic panoramic view of the Alps.

- Ski in ski out resort
- Access to the amazing 3 valleys ski domain: 373 miles of slopes
- Wide array of thrilling and innovative snow sports including speed-riding, mountain biking, boardercross, sledding.
- You hit the pristine slopes while we prepare the fondue.

PART 7 / EN CONDITIONS D'EXAMEN

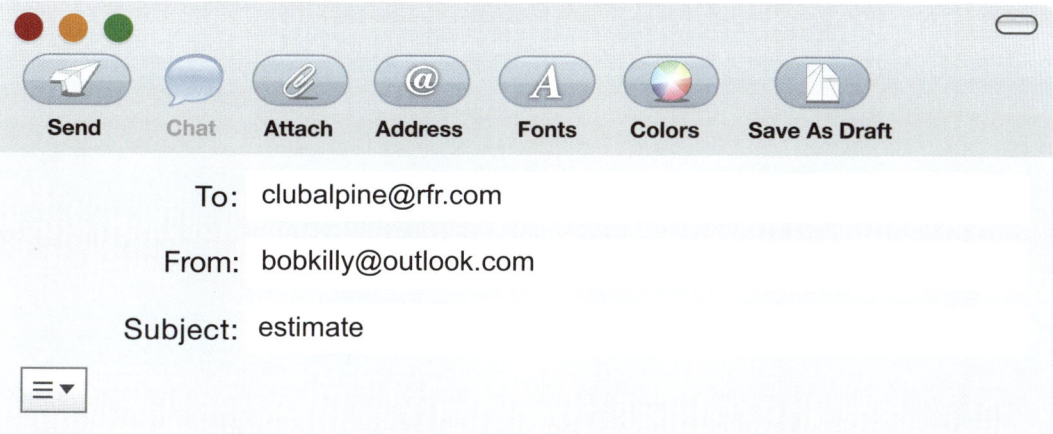

Date: April 2nd

Hi!

I am Bob and I live in Colorado State. My wife and I normally take our vacations in the Rockies at Beaver Creek. But as we were about to book our next winter holidays at our travel agency we saw your ad and we thought: "Why not have a ski experience in the French Alps for a change?"

These are just holiday plans but to take it more seriously I need fare information. Could you please send us your best offers as well as a detailed estimate on those bases?

Date: next year, from March 7th 2019, to March 14th 2019.
No transport.
One child under 5 but we don't know yet if she will be part of our trip.
High level in skiing.

I look forward to hearing your reply.

PART 7 / EN CONDITIONS D'EXAMEN

CLUB ALPINE
Grande Rue - 73440 Saint Martin

April 2nd, 2018

Hello Bob,

Thank you for your interest in our ski resort and we hope we will meet your expectations.

As I understand, you are both experienced skiers I think that Val Tho will suit you perfectly. (I enclose brochures so that you can see the amazing slopes you will soon hurtle!)

You are also so right to ask for an estimate now because with an early booking you can slide into big savings! Please find below our best offer:

Accommodation: Room Club: 1 to 3 guests (39 m2)

Date: based on 7 nights from 7 March, 2019 to 14 March, 2019.

Children under 6 pay half price of the discount price.

The normal price would be $299 per night per adult but if you book before April 13th the price will be $189 per night per adult.

So your all-inclusive vacation (see details in the brochure) in Val Tho will be: 7 nights x $378 = $2,646.

(if you come with your toddler you will have to add $661.50)

The whole staff from Club Alpine is waiting for you to make these holidays the time of your life.

PART 7 / EN CONDITIONS D'EXAMEN

20 What do we know about Bob Killy?

a. ☐ He has already skied in the Alps.

b. ☐ He has already booked with Club Alpine.

c. ☐ He is a regular skier in the US.

d. ☐ He is fed up with skiing the the Rockies.

21 Why should the Killies book now?

a. ☐ Because it is already snowing.

b. ☐ Because early booking is money-saving.

c. ☐ Because the Alps is the best ski resort in the world.

d. ☐ Because they will have time to fill up their piggy bank.

22 What will the total amount be if their daughter comes?

a. ☐ $2,646

b. ☐ $661.50

c. ☐ $4,739

d. ☐ $3,307.50

23 What is not included in the All-inclusive offer?

a. ☐ Hard liquor.

b. ☐ The nursery club.

c. ☐ The ski passes.

d. ☐ All you can eat buffet.

→ **Voir réponses page 109.**

PART 7 / EN CONDITIONS D'EXAMEN

 Why are the French Alps the best ski resort in the world?

a. ☐ The panoramic view is stunning.

b. ☐ French food is the best.

c. ☐ It is the largest ski area in the world.

d. ☐ Ski passes are affordable.

➜ **Voir réponses page 109.**

Réponses
de cette mise en conditions

1. b.
2. c.
3. b.
4. d.
5. c.
6. a.
7. c.
8. b.
9. d.
10. b.
11. d.
12. c.
13. d.
14. a.
15. b.
16. b.
17. c.
18. d.
19. b.
20. c.
21. b.
22. d.
23. a.
24. c.

Annexes

LES VERBES IRRÉGULIERS

Les verbes irréguliers

Infinitif	Prétérit	Participe passé	Traduction
abide	abode	abode	*souffrir, supporter*
arise	arose	arisen	*survenir*
awake	awoke	awoken	*se réveiller*
be	was, were	been	*être*
bear	bore	borne / born	*porter / supporter*
beat	beat	beaten	*battre*
become	became	become	*devenir*
beget	begat / begot	begotten	*engendrer*
begin	began	begun	*commencer*
bend	bent	bent	*plier / se courber*
bereave	bereft / bereaved	bereft / bereaved	*déposséder / priver*
bet	bet	bet	*parier*
bid	bid / bade	bid / bidden	*offrir*
bite	bit	bitten	*mordre*
bleed	bled	bled	*saigner*
blow	blew	blown	*souffler / gonfler*
break	broke	broken	*casser*
breed	bred	bred	*élever (des animaux)*
bring	brought	brought	*apporter*
broadcast	broadcast	broadcast	*diffuser / émettre*
build	built	built	*construire*
burn	burnt / burned	burnt / burned	*brûler*
burst	burst	burst	*éclater*
buy	bought	bought	*acheter*
can	could	could	*pouvoir*
cast	cast	cast	*jeter / distribuer (rôles)*
catch	caught	caught	*attraper*
chide	chid	chiden	*gronder*
choose	chose	chosen	*choisir*
cling	clung	clung	*s'accrocher*
clothe	clad / clothed	clad / clothed	*habiller / recouvrir*
come	came	come	*venir*
cost	cost	cost	*coûter*
creep	crept	crept	*ramper*
cut	cut	cut	*couper*
deal	dealt	dealt	*distribuer*
dig	dug	dug	*creuser*

LES VERBES IRRÉGULIERS

dive	dived	dived / dove	*plonger*
do	did	done	*faire*
draw	drew	drawn	*dessiner / tirer*
dream	dreamt / dreamed	dreamt / dreamed	*rêver*
drink	drank	drunk	*boire*
drive	drove	driven	*conduire*
dwell	dwelt	dwelt / dwelled	*habiter*
eat	ate	eaten	*manger*
fall	fell	fallen	*tomber*
feed	fed	fed	*nourrir*
feel	felt	felt	*se sentir / ressentir*
fight	fought	fought	*se battre*
find	found	found	*trouver*
flee	fled	fled	*s'enfuir*
fling	flung	flung	*lancer*
fly	flew	flown	*voler*
forbid	forbade	forbidden	*interdire*
forecast	forecast	forecast	*prévoir*
forget	forgot	forgotten / forgot	*oublier*
forgive	forgave	forgiven	*pardonner*
forsake	forsook	forsaken	*abandonner*
forsee	foresaw	foresawn	*prévoir / pressentir*
freeze	froze	frozen	*geler*
get	got	gotten / got	*obtenir*
give	gave	given	*donner*
go	went	gone	*aller*
grind	ground	ground	*moudre / opprimer*
grow	grew	grown	*grandir / pousser*
hang	hung	hung	*tenir / pendre*
have	had	had	*avoir*
hear	heard	heard	*entendre*
hide	hid	hidden	*cacher*
hit	hit	hit	*taper / appuyer*
hold	held	held	*tenir*
hurt	hurt	hurt	*blesser*
keep	kept	kept	*garder*
kneel	knelt / knelled	knelt / kneeled	*s'agenouiller*
know	knew	known	*connaître / savoir*
lay	laid	laid	*poser*
lead	led	led	*mener / guider*
lean	leant / leaned	leant / leaned	*s'incliner / se pencher*
leap	leapt / leaped	leapt / leaped	*sauter / bondir*
learn	learnt	learnt	*apprendre*
leave	left	left	*laisser / quitter / partir*
lend	lent	lent	*prêter*
let	let	let	*permettre / louer*
lie	lay	lain	*s'allonger*

LES VERBES IRRÉGULIERS

light	lit / lighted	lit / lighted	*allumer*
lose	lost	lost	*perdre*
make	made	made	*fabriquer*
mean	meant	meant	*signifier*
meet	met	met	*rencontrer*
mow	mowed	mowed / mown	*tondre*
offset	offset	offset	*compenser*
overcome	overcame	overcome	*surmonter*
partake	partook	partaken	*prendre part à*
pay	paid	paid	*payer*
plead	pled / pleaded		*pled / pleaded*
preset	preset	preset	*programmer*
prove	proved	proven / proved	*prouver*
put	put	put	*mettre*
quit	quit	quit	*quitter*
read	read	read	*lire*
relay	relaid	relaid	*relayer*
rend	rent	rent	*déchirer*
rid	rid	rid	*débarrasser*
ride	rode	ridden	*monter (vélo, cheval)*
ring	rang	rung	*sonner / téléphoner*
rise	rose	risen	*lever*
run	ran	run	*courir*
saw	saw / sawed	sawn / sawed	*scier*
say	said	said	*dire*
see	saw	seen	*voir*
seek	sought	sought	*chercher*
sell	sold	sold	*vendre*
send	sent	sent	*envoyer*
set	set	set	*fixer*
shake	shook	shaken	*secouer*
shed	shed	shed	*répandre / laisser tomber*
shine	shone	shone	*briller*
shoe	shod	shod	*chausser*
shoot	shot	shot	*tirer / fusiller*
show	showed	shown	*montrer*
shut	shut	shut	*fermer*
sing	sang	sung	*chanter*
sink	sank / sunk	sunk / sunken	*couler*
sit	sat	sat	*s'asseoir*
slay	slew	slain	*tuer*
sleep	slept	slept	*dormir*
slide	slid	slid	*glisser*
slink	slunk / slinked	slunk / slinked	*s'en aller furtivement*
slit	slit	slit	*fendre*
smell	smelt	smelt	*sentir*
sow	sowed	sown / sowed	*semer*

LES VERBES IRRÉGULIERS

speak	spoke	spoken	*parler*
speed	sped	sped	*aller vite*
spell	spelt	spelt	*épeler / orthographier*
spend	spent	spent	*dépenser / passer du temps*
spill	spilt / spilled	spilt / spilled	*renverser*
spin	spun	spun	*tourner / faire tourner*
spit	spat / spit	spat / spit	*cracher*
split	split	split	*fendre*
spoil	spoilt	spoilt	*gâcher / gâter*
spread	spread	spread	*répandre*
spring	sprang	sprung	*surgir / jaillir / bondir*
stand	stood	stood	*être debout*
steal	stole	stolen	*voler / dérober*
stick	stuck	stuck	*coller*
sting	stung	stung	*piquer*
stink	stank	stunk	*puer*
strew	strewed	strewn / strewed	*éparpiller*
strike	struck	stricken / struck	*frapper*
strive	strove	striven	*s'efforcer*
swear	swore	sworn	*jurer*
sweat	sweat / sweated	sweat / sweated	*suer*
sweep	swept	swept	*balayer*
swell	swelled	swollen / swelled	*gonfler / enfler*
swim	swam	swum	*nager*
swing	swung	swung	*se balancer*
take	took	taken	*prendre*
teach	taught	taught	*enseigner*
tear	tore	torn	*déchirer*
tell	told	told	*dire / raconter*
think	thought	thought	*penser*
thrive	throve / thrived	thriven / thrived	*prospérer*
throw	threw	thrown	*jeter*
thrust	thrust	thrust	*enfoncer*
tread	trod	trodden	*piétiner quelque chose*
typeset	typeset	typeset	*composer*
undergo	underwent	undergone	*subir*
understand	understood	understood	*comprendre*
wake	woke	woken	*réveiller*
wear	wore	worn	*porter (avoir sur soi)*
weep	wept	wept	*pleurer*
wet	wet / wetted	wet / wetted	*mouiller*
win	won	won	*gagner*
wind	wound	wound	*enrouler / remonter*
withdraw	withdrew	withdrawn	*se retirer*
wring	wrung	wrung	*tordre*
write	wrote	written	*écrire*

LES VERBES IRRÉGULIERS

Les verbes irréguliers dont le prétérit et le participe passé sont identiques

Infinitif	Prétérit	Participe passé	Traduction
to bend	bent	bent	(se) courber
to bind	bound	bound	lier, relier
to bleed	bled	bled	saigner
to breed	bred	bred	élever (enfants, bétail)
to bring	brought	brought	apporter
to build	built	built	construire
to burn	burnt	burnt	brûler
to buy	bought	bought	acheter
to catch	caught	caught	attraper
to creep	crept	crept	ramper
to deal	dealt	dealt	distribuer
to dig	dug	dug	creuser
to dream	dreamt	dreamt	rêver
to feed	fed	fed	nourrir
to feel	felt	felt	(se) sentir, ressentir
to fight	fought	fought	se battre, combattre
to find	found	found	trouver
to flee	fled	fled	s'enfuir
to get	got	got	obtenir
to hang	hung	hung	pendre, accrocher
to have	had	had	avoir
to hear	heard	heard	entendre
to hold	held	held	tenir
to keep	kept	kept	garder
to kneel	knelt	knelt	s'agenouiller
to lay	laid	laid	poser à plat
to lead	led	led	mener, guider

LES VERBES IRRÉGULIERS

Infinitif	Prétérit	Participe passé	Traduction
to lean	leant	leant	s'appuyer
to leap	leapt	leapt	sauter
to learn	learnt	learnt	apprendre
to leave	left	left	quitter, partir
to lend	lent	lent	prêter
to light	lit	lit	allumer
to lose	lost	lost	perdre
to make	made	made	faire, fabriquer
to mean	meant	meant	vouloir dire, signifier
to meet	met	met	rencontrer
to pay	paid	paid	payer
to say	said	said	dire
to seek	sought	sought	chercher, rechercher
to sell	sold	sold	vendre
to send	sent	sent	envoyer
to shine	shone	shone	briller
to shoot	shot	shot	tirer, tourner un film
to sit	sat	sat	s'asseoir
to sleep	slept	slept	dormir
to smell	smelt	smelt	sentir (odeur)
to spell	spelt	spelt	épeler
to spend	spent	spent	passer son temps, dépenser son argent
to spill	spilt	spilt	renverser (liquide)
to spit	spat	spat	cracher
to spoil	spoilt	spoilt	gâcher, gâter
to stand	stood	stood	se tenir debout
to stick	stuck	stuck	coller
to strike	struck	struck	frapper
to sweep	swept	swept	balayer
to swing	swung	swung	(se) balancer
to teach	taught	taught	enseigner
to tell	told	told	dire, raconter
to think	thought	thought	penser
to understand	understood	understood	comprendre
to weep	wept	wept	pleurer
to win	won	won	gagner

LES VERBES IRRÉGULIERS

Trois formes identiques

Infinitif	Prétérit	Participe passé	Traduction
to bet	bet	bet	*parier*
to burst	burst	burst	*éclater*
to cost	cost	cost	*coûter*
to cut	cut	cut	*couper*
to hit	hit	hit	*frapper, atteindre*
to hurt	hurt	hurt	*faire mal*
to let	let	let	*laisser, permettre*
to put	put	put	*mettre, poser*
to read	read	read	*lire*
to set	set	set	*fixer, placer*
to shut	shut	shut	*fermer*
to split	split	split	*fendre*
to spread	spread	spread	*répandre, étaler*
to upset	upset	upset	*bouleverser*

Deux formes identiques

Infinitif	Prétérit	Participe passé	Traduction
to beat	beat	beaten	*battre*
to become	became	become	*devenir*
to come	came	come	*venir*
to overcome	overcame	overcome	*surmonter*
to run	ran	run	*courir*

LES VERBES IRRÉGULIERS

Liste complémentaire

Infinitif	Prétérit	Participe passé	Traduction
to abide	abode	abode	*endurer*
to bear	bore	borne / born	*porter / supporter*
to befall	befell	befallen	*advenir*
to beget	begot	begotten	*engendrer*
to behold	beheld	beheld	*apercevoir*
to bereave	bereaved	bereft	*déposséder*
to beseech	besought	besought	*implorer*
to bid	bade	bidden	*ordonner*
to bid	bid	bid	*faire une offre*
to chide	chid	chid	*réprimander*
to clothe	clothed / clad	clothed / clad	*vêtir*
to crow	crowed	crowed	*gazouiller*
to dare	dared / durst	dared / durst	*oser*
to dwell	dwelled / dwelt	dwelled / dwelt	*demeurer*
to fling	flung	flung	*lancer*
to forbear	forbore	forborne	*s'abstenir*
to forsake	forsook	forsaken	*délaisser*
to gild	gilt	gilt	*dorer*
to gird	girded / girt	girded / girt	*ceindre*
to hew	hewed	hown	*équarrir*
to knit	knit	knit	*tricoter*
to lean	leant	leant	*s'appuyer*
to mow	mowed	mown	*tondre (pelouse)*
to rend	rent	rent	*fendre*
to sew	sewed	sewed / sewn	*coudre*
to shear	sheared / shore	sheared / shorn	*cisailler*
to shed	shed	shed	*dépouiller*
to shoe	shoed / shod	shoed / shod	*être chaussé / ferré*
to shrink	shrank	shrunk	*rétrécir*
to slay	slew	slain	*tuer*
to slide	slid	slid	*glisser*

LES VERBES IRRÉGULIERS

Infinitif	Prétérit	Participe passé	Traduction
to sling	slung	slung	*lancer*
to slink	slunk	slunk	*se retirer furtivement*
to slit	slit	slit	*inciser*
to smite	smote	smitten	*châtier*
to speed	speeded / sped	speeded / sped	*aller vite*
to spin	spun	spun	*faire tourner*
to stink	stank / stunk	stunk	*puer*
to strew	strewed	strewed / strewn	*éparpiller*
to stride	strode	stridden	*marcher à grandes enjambées*
to strike	struck	struck	*frapper*
to string	strung	strung	*ficeler*
to strive	strove	striven	*s'efforcer*
to thrive	thrived / throve	thrived / thriven	*être florissant*
to thrust	thrust	thrust	*pousser violemment*
to weave	wove	woven	*tisser*
to wet	wetted / wet	wetted / wet	*mouiller*
to wind	wound	wound	*embobiner*
to wring	wrung	wrung	*tordre*

Glossaire

- **Transport / les transports**

Air field: *terrain d'aviation*

Aircraft: *avion*

Baggage room (US): *consigne*

Barge: *péniche*

Branch line: *ligne secondaire*

Cargo: *une cargaison*

Cattle truck: *wagon à bestiaux*

Conductor: *contrôleur*

Fare: *tarif*

Freight train (US): *train de marchandises*

Goods train (GB): *train de marchandises*

High-speed train: *train à grande vitesse*

Highway (US): *autoroute*

Left-luggage office (GB): *consigne*

Lifeboat: *canot de sauvetage*

Lighthouse: *phare*

Lock: *écluse*

Long vehicle: *convoi exceptionnel*

Lorry (GB): *camion*

Motorway (GB): *autoroute*

One-way ticket: *aller simple*

Pass: *abonnement*

Return ticket: *aller-retour*

Sailing boat: *voilier*

Ship: *vaisseau, navire*

Shuttle: *navette*

Suburban train: *train de banlieue*

Supertanker: *un pétrolier*

Through flight: *vol direct*

To land: *atterrir*

To pull in: *entrer en gare*

To punch: *composter*

To stop over: *faire escale*

To take off: *décoller*

Toll: *péage*

Tow-truck: *dépanneuse*

Truck (US): *camion*

- **Business correspondence / communication professionnelle**

By return of post: *par retour de courrier*

Complaint letter: *lettre de réclamation*

Estimate: *devis*

Follow up letter: *lettre de relance*

Inconvenience: *ennuis, dérangements*

Item: *article*

Legal action: *poursuite judiciaire*

GLOSSAIRE

Letter of application: *lettre de candidature*

Letterhead: *en-tête*

On behalf of: *de la part de*

Parcel: *colis*

Sample: *échantillon*

Schedule: *horaire*

Stationary: *papeterie*

Suitable: *qui convient*

To acknowledge receipt: *accuser réception*

To agree to: *convenir*

To book an order: *enregistrer une commande*

To carry out an order: *exécuter une commande*

To come into force: *entrer en vigueur*

To dispatch / to consign: *expédier*

To enclose / to attach: *joindre un document*

To forward: *faire suivre*

To meet a deadine: *honorer un délai*

To stamp: *oblitérer*

To take steps: *faire des démarches*

To weigh: *peser*

Trial: *essai*

Unforeseen: *imprévu*

Waybill: *bordereau d'expédition*

Weight: *le poids*

• **Internet / Internet**

Acces data: *accès aux données*

Access provider: *fournisseur d'accès*

Bug: *panne*

Data sharing: *partage des données*

IT: *l'informatique*

Junk mail / spam: *mail indésirable*

Network: *réseau*

Software: *logiciel*

To backup: *sauvegarder*

To browse: *naviguer, surfer*

To crack: *décoder, décrypter*

To display: *afficher à l'écran*

To download: *télécharger*

To log off: *se déconnecter*

To log on: *se connecter*

To remove:
retirer, enlever

User-friendly: *convivial*

• **Upward trends / tendances haussières**

A bull market: *Bourse en hausse*

To bolster: *renforcer, soutenir*

To boom: *exploser*

To boost: *booster*

To enhance: *étendre*

To go up: *monter, augmenter*

To grow: *grandir*

To increase: *augmenter*

To peak: *atteindre son plus haut niveau*

To rise: *s'élever*

To soar: *monter en flèche*

To swell: *grossir, enfler*

To thrive: *être prospère*

To upgrade: *améliorer*

GLOSSAIRE

- **Downward trends / tendances baissières**

A bear market: *Bourse en baisse*

A crash: *une faillite*

A drop: *une chute*

A fall: *une chute*

A slump: *chute brutale, effondrement*

To abate: *baisser*

To decline: *décliner*

To decrease: *décroître*

To diminish: *diminuer*

To drop: *chuter*

To dwindle: *diminuer*

To lessen: *diminuer*

To shrink: *rétrécir*

- **Money / l'argent**

A grant: *une subvention*

An amount: *un montant*

Banknote, a bill: *un billet de banque*

Bonus: *prime*

Cash: *espèces, numéraire*

Change: *monnaie*

Coin: *une pièce de monnaie*

Currency: *devise, monnaie*

Earnings: *les gains*

Expenses: *les dépenses*

Income: *revenu*

Investor: *investisseur*

Litigation: *contentieux*

Loss: *une perte*

No pain, no gain: *on n'a rien sans rien*

Overdraft: *découvert à la banque*

Profits: *les gains*

Raw materials: *matières premières*

Savings: *l'épargne*

Taxes: *les impôts*

Thrifty: *économe*

To amount to: *s'élever à*

To bail out: *renflouer*

To borrow: *emprunter*

To buy on credit: *acheter à crédit*

To earn: *gagner de l'argent*

To grant: *accorder*

To lend: *prêter*

To owe money: *devoir de l'argent*

To pay back: *rembourser*

To pay in several instalments: *payer en plusieurs fois*

To pay off: *payer ses dettes*

To save: *économiser*

To spend: *dépenser*

To squander: *dilapider*

To thrift: *économiser*

To waste: *gaspiller*

Turnover: *le roulement, chiffre d'affaires*

- **Production / la production**

A contractor: *un entrepreneur*

Brand: *une marque*

Breakthrough: *une avancée, une percée*

Competitiveness: *la concurrence*

Competitor: *concurrent*

GLOSSAIRE

Goods, wares: *les marchandises*

Handmade: *fabriqué à la main*

Item : *article*

Made on demand: *fabriqué à la demande*

Manufacture: *fabriquer*

Mass-produced: *fabriqué à la chaîne*

Out of stock: *en rupture de stock*

Output: *la production*

Registered trademark: *marque déposée*

Shortage: *pénurie*

Stock depletion: *épuisement des stocks*

Subcontractor: *sous-traitant*

To be in stock: *disponible, avoir en stock*

To supply: *approvisionner*

To target: *cibler*

Yield: *rendement*

Consumerism: *le consumérisme*

Fad: *lubie*

Launch price: *prix de lancement*

Mall: *centre commercial*

Priceless: *inestimable*

Shop, store: *magasin*

To bargain: *marchander*

To claim damages: *demander des dommages et intérêts*

To provide: *fournir*

Unaffordable: *inabordable*

• Consumption / la consommation

A bargain: *une bonne affaire*

Affordable: *abordable*

After sales service: *service après-vente*

Best value for money: *un bon rapport qualité-prix*

Bonanza: *une aubaine*

Branch: *une succursale*

Brand, trademark: *une marque*

Cheap: *bon marché*

Clearance sale: *une liquidation*

Consumer goods, durables: *biens de consommation*

Consumer survey: *une étude de consommateurs*

Consumer trend: *une tendance de consommation*

• Employment and employees / l'emploi et les employés

Application: *une demande*

Apprentice: *un apprenti*

Apprenticeship: *apprentissage*

Blue collar worker: *un ouvrier*

Craftsman: *artisan*

CV / résumé: *curriculum vitae*

Excecutive: *cadre*

Free lance / self employed: *travailleur libéral*

Full time / part time: *à temps plein / partiel*

Graduate: *diplôme universitaire*

Intern: *stagiaire*

Job interview: *entretien d'embauche*

Jobless: *sans emploi*

Low-paid job: *travail mal rétribué*

Odd jobs: *petits boulots*

Paid leave: *congés payés*

Perks: *avantages*

GLOSSAIRE

Skilled / unskilled: *qualifié / non qualifié*

Temporary work: *travail intérimaire*

To apply for: *postuler*

To appoint somebody: *nommer quelqu'un*

Underground economy: *économie parallèle*

Wages: *salaire*

Well-paid job: *un emploi bien rémunéré*

White collar worker: *un employé de bureau*

Work overtime: *faire des heures supplémentaires*

Workaholic: *bourreau de travail*

• Vacations and holidays / les vacances

Accommodation: *logement*

All inclusive: *pension complète*

Bank holiday: *jour férié*

Book: *réserver*

Check in / check out: *arriver / repartir*

Day off: *un jour de congé*

Guesthouse: *maison d'hôte*

Holidaymaker: *vacancier*

Mass tourism: *le tourisme de masse*

No vacancies: *complet*

Sea resort: *station balnéaire*

Ski resort: *station de ski*

• Greetings / les formules de politesse

Best regards: *salutations*

Dear Madam: *chère madame*

Dear Mr Smith: *cher monsieur Smith*

Dear Sir: *cher monsieur*

Feel free to contact me: *n'hésitez pas à me contacter*

Further to: *suite à*

Hereby attached: *ci-joint*

I am writing to let you know: *je vous écris pour vous informer*

I'd be grateful if you could: *je vous serais reconnaissant si vous pouviez*

I'd like to express my gratitude for your help: *j'aimerais vous remercier de votre aide*

If you need more additional assistance, please contact me: *si vous avez besoin d'aide, merci de me contacter*

If you need more information: *si vous avez besoin d'informations complémentaires*

Kind regards: *cordialement*

miss: *mademoiselle*

Mr: *monsieur*

Mrs: *madame*

Ms: *une dame. Aucune indication sur son statut marital.*

Please find attached: *veuillez trouver ci-joint*

Please find below: *veuillez trouver ci-dessous*

Please find enclosed: *vous trouverez ci-joint*

Thank you for your availibility: *merci de votre disponibilité*

Thank you for your consideration on the matter: *merci de votre attention*

To whom it may concern: *à qui de droit*

We are delighted to tell you that: *nous sommes ravis de vous annoncer que*

We regret to inform you: *nous sommes au regret de vous informer*

With reference to: *en ce qui concerne*

GLOSSAIRE

Would you mind giving me more details?: *pourriez-vous me donner plus de détails ?*

Yours faithfully: *je vous prie d'agréer l'expression de mes salutations distinguées*

Yours sincerely: *Je vous prie d'agréer l'expression de ma haute considération*

• Measures of capacity and weight / les mesures de capacité et de poids

1 pint GB: *0,57 litre*

1 pint US: *0,47 litre*

1 gallon GB: *4,54 litres*

1 gallon US: *3,78 litres*

1 oz: *28,35 grammes*

1 pound: *453,6 grammes*

1 stone: *6,35 kilos*

• Temperatures / les températures

10 °C: *50°F*

0 °C: *32°F*

• Linear measures / mesures de longueur

1 inch: *2,54 centimètres*

1 foot: *30,48 centimètres*

1 yard: *91,44 centimètres*

1 mile: *1 609 mètres*

TABLEAU D'AUTOÉVALUATION

Bravo, vous êtes venu à bout de ce cahier ! Il est temps à présent de faire le point sur vos compétences et de comptabiliser les icônes afin de procéder à l'évaluation finale. Reportez le sous-total de chaque partie dans les cases ci-dessous, puis additionnez-les afin d'obtenir le nombre final d'icônes dans chaque couleur. Enfin, découvrez vos résultats !

Part 5 Incomplete sentences ....

Part 6 Complete the text ....

Part 7 Comprehension ....

Total, toutes parties confondues ....

Vous avez obtenu une majorité de...

Good job!
Vous pouvez vous présenter
à la certification !

Keep going…
Vous pouvez encore progresser ! Refaites les exercices qui vous ont donné du fil à retordre !

Don't give up!
Reprenez l'ensemble de l'ouvrage et comprenez vos erreurs.

CRÉDITS

Crédits iconographiques :

iStock : Qvasimodo : 22 ; **Shutterstock :** ADE2013 : 126 ; Aleutie : 42b ; Anastasia_B : 123 ; AriSys : 69 ; Dacian G : 122 ; Evellean : 54 ; Fay Francevna : 13 ; forden : 35 ; Fred Ho : 18 ; getfile : 33hd ; GoodVector : 3 ; graphic-line : 15 ; happymay : 21b ; Henry Olden : 59 ; HieroGraphic : 91 ; Incomible : 75 ; jesadaphorn : 17, 19hg, 31, 32, 38, 78 ; Lindarks : 124 ; Lucky Team Studio : 21 (abeille) ; Macrovector : 42 ; Marharyta Pavliuk : 55 ; mari.nl : 16 ; Mascha Tace : 5, 56 ; Meder Lorant : 67 ; melissa held : 68 ; mhatzapa : 25m ; Millena : 23, 26 ; MSSA : 46 ; MyClipArtStore.com : 41 ; Oceans : 12hd ; Olga1818 : 18b, 20, 33b ; robuart : 48 ; Rudie Strummer : 25 ; Seita : 61 ; subarashii21 : 24m ; venimo : 36 ; Visual Generation : 11, 27 ; yoshi-5 : 34 ; yuriytsirkunov : 19, 43 ; Yuyula : 121 ; **Vecteezy :** ayaankabir : 44 ; pumashoeme : 45, 47 ; swayaway1 : 12b ; blackfrog714 : 57 ; designkeptme : 95, 96 ; dollyheidi : 82 ; dumbmichael : 80 (fond) ; eryprihananto : 91(café) ; freevector : 89 ; insanity100 : 82 (couteau) ; KoiStudio : 37 ; lavarmsg : 6, 84 ; MacDaddy : 98, 105 ; MiniStock : 24b, 53, 63, 90 ; momentbloom : 70 ; veernavya : 104, 106 ; watchtaxinyc : 62 ; xiayamoon : 60 ; yoosillyone : 58, 58b ; zhaolifang : 76, 78m.

Création et réalisation : Lunedit, lunedit.com
Couverture : Allright

© 2018, Assimil
Dépôt légal : avril 2018
N° d'édition : 4234 - mars 2023

ISBN : 978-2-7005-0817-8

www.assimil.com

Imprimé en Roumanie par Master Print